THE GIRL

(A memoir of divine guidance and triumph)

Written by

Sandra Mbeyi

Published by

El Printing

CONTENTS

ACKNOWLEDGEMENT

First, I acknowledge Abba, my ever-present help. The one who chose my clueless self and showed me grace, mercy, and love.

I am grateful for my husband, who is a physical manifestation of Abba's lavish love for me. My children, who are both Abba's love expressed to me.

I am eternally grateful for my family, who are my rock and world.

I am thankful for my mom's strength, tenacity, and doggedness. I have no idea where I'd be without my family's (Mom, Marvin, Kevin, and Padre) support.

DEDICATION

Dedicated to Abba.

To every young girl trying to find her path and purpose.

To every young girl doubtful of life, God's mercy, finding love, and drowning in sin, I was you, and I see you. Jesus loves you.

NOTE

This book was written to inspire every woman out there and to remind you that God has not given up on you (and He won't), so don't give up on yourself.

INTRODUCTION

When my brothers, Marvin and Kevin, and I left the shores of Nigeria for the United States of America to meet our dad, it felt like it would be an adventure to relish and a place to love. After being separated from him for a long time, we felt this might be the beginning of something great for the family. However, it turned out to be one of our worst nightmares.

The country's citizens did not haunt us, and neither were we troubled by strangers. On the contrary, most of our challenges resulted from our dad's actions and inactions. Consequently, I was bruised, depressed, angry, and had to step into a strange world at a time I shouldn't have. I watched as my life became a shadow of itself and something I could no longer recognise. In my teen years, I had to become my brothers' mother, provider, mentor, and protector while still being their sister.

As the first child, I had nobody I could lean on apart from God, and I was close to dying on many occasions. There were times I was a whisker away from the jaws of death, but God, the King of Kings, would always come to my rescue. My life became the epitome of God's grace and miracles. Without God's guidance and intervention, I wouldn't be here today. God used my situation to prove to me that He exists. Thankfully, I held on to Him without letting go.

The truth is that our life's trajectory and the major part of what makes us who we are were predetermined by our parents and those before us. Our circumstances are sometimes a product of other people's actions and decisions. Even our biological makeup isn't determined by us but by others. This is why we must commit every decision we make in God's hands, even before we make them, because our sight can only see so far, but total faith in God can see beyond where our sights can reach.

My mom married my dad a year before I was born. She said he was a lovely man at the time, and he made her believe in love. He was as loving as he was as caring.

Less than a year into their marriage, I was their first child and a product of that blossoming love. I must confess that I felt a bit of that love when we were in Nigeria as one big happy family. My dad was a hardworking and devoted man who was always willing to provide everything his family needed. However, everything changed when he travelled to the United States of America. It became the beginning of a new chapter of our life—one that would scar every family member for years. My dad's decision altered our family dynamics and almost crumbled it.

As a result of their marriage's trajectory, I swore that, with the grace and mercy of God, mine would be different, and it would be a reference to God's idea of marriage, and it would glorify Him. I learnt from their lesson and prayed to be the opposite of whatever they had. I vowed to stay aligned with the will of God regarding marriage. I also promised to commit my marriage to the Lord's hands to make it safe and beautiful.

In this book, you will learn much about God, marriage, parenting, miracles, strength, resilience, and what a person can achieve when they say no to all life's challenges. It will make you scream, cry, and wonder if it is true. But brace yourself up because this is real.

This is my story! This is my truth!!

CHAPTER 1

THE GENESIS

"One thing about our life is that it doesn't begin the day we are born. It has its roots years before that very day."

Sandra Mbeyi

I remember when I took a train for the first time. It was a beautiful ride. I sat beside a chitty-chatty passenger who made the ride even more memorable. There's something I've learned about trains. They tend to move with a uniform velocity when they are in motion. Unlike cars, they do not brake or slow down suddenly during a journey. Once they start, they don't stop until a predetermined point (station). However, cars can stop anywhere, anytime, and for almost any reason.

Interestingly, I'm not here to talk about physics and how its principles work. Rather, I'm here to talk about chemistry. Not the one you were taught in school, no. I'm talking about the one you learned as you went further in life. I'm talking about the chemistry of love. Yes, love! That powerful force, the greatest commandment, and that energy that can hurt and heal. Yes, that's right, love. It is one word many women are always happy to hear. On the other hand, some women don't want to hear it at all. It irks them, and I think I know why it does.

I have noticed that the chemistry of love behaves more like the physics of cars than trains. It will start slowly, go fast, and slow down when someone makes it. Its speed can also be increased, unlike trains that maintain one almost all through their journey.

This phenomenon has made me wonder how two people who once loved each other dearly suddenly do not anymore. How does it happen? When they are at the full speed of love, what halts them? Why does love behave like a car and not just go smoothly like a train to its destination? Nonetheless, in cars, there's a driver who controls the movement, but in trains, the tracks determine the direction, which is why love behaves like a car. The people in it are the ones who determine the road they travel on, which could be the sweet, loving road or the one filled with the potholes of strife, chaos, and violence. Some even change direction in the middle of the journey. They begin on the road of love, and suddenly, they drive themselves into the chaotic and violent one.

However, I'm not here to talk about trains and cars but to tell you my story. It is a story that began with love and continued in it, but somehow came a devastating detour, which I will let you in on.

James Hauenstein said,

> "Until the heart can see the future of the person you fall in love with, love will always be blind."

That's the tragedy, James; nobody can see the future. Consequently, we can only judge our beloved by what they are today. Furthermore, as I said earlier, this isn't a story about cars, trains, or physics; it is rather a love story, or, should I say, the lack thereof. Well, it began with love but never ended with it. Love, not gravity, is the greatest force on earth. It can decide to take you up and never come down.

This is my story. A story that began before I was born but would later become my tragedy.

The story begins

As I began writing this book, I realised that I must do justice to it by going back to the beginning, and that beginning was before I was born. I find myself engulfed in a whirl of memories that take me back to when life seemed to unfold like a meticulously crafted romance novel as I write about the beginnings of my parent's love story. It was different from the conventional way of doing things then. It was bold and curious, depicting nothing but someone certain about his desires. It was prophetic, electric, emphatic, and ecstatic.

> *One thing about our life is that it doesn't begin the day we are born; it has its roots years before that very day.*

My mother's recollection of their initial meeting is like stepping into a painting, where colours blend seamlessly to create a masterpiece of serendipity and destiny. She paints a vivid picture of that fateful day. Her eyes alight with the fire of reminiscence as she recounts the scene with intricate detail. Her eyes glistened as she told us how beautiful their beginning was, but as she continued, the passion in her eyes, like the love she had shared with my dad, dissolved, and it was evident in her voice.

One thing about our life is that it doesn't begin the day we are born. It has its roots years before that very day. Every decision our parents made and every choice their parents (our grandparents) made all combine to form the foundation of our life. Every individual you see on earth is a product of choice not made by them. We are all a product of someone else's decisions. My mom made a choice many years and I, even unborn at the time, would later pay a part of the price. Some decisions our parents make in life are so steep they can't pay it all in a lifetime. So, we, their children, must pay a part of the price.

The first meeting between my mom and the man who would eventually become my dad was at her friend's house. She had gone to visit her friend when he saw her. He approached her and told her how beautiful she was and how much he liked her. However, my mom was from a strict background, and her siblings always counselled her to avoid anything related to men and love like it was a plague. She was young, naïve, and beautiful, making her the perfect prey for men—good and bad. As a result of that, she told him off. Like the night, he vanished, but only for a while. Remember, the night will always come back, no matter how bright the day is.

For almost two years, he never disturbed her again until one morning that would change everyone's lives, both living and unborn.

It was a sunny afternoon, the air alive with the melody of laughter and the gentle hum of conversations. Amidst the teeming earthly population, two souls, oblivious to the fate that awaits them, gravitated towards each other with an irresistible pull, like magnets drawn together by an unseen force.

My mother was a young girl preparing to retake her High School final exams and the University Entrance Examination. At the time, her education was her only desire. Give her a pen and a piece of paper to write all she wished and education would have been the only thing on the list. She admired and loved it with everything in her. However, fate was about to change her desires and bestow a new one.

A friend once quipped, "Life doesn't give you what you want or deserve; it just gives you whatever it has in reserve." She was right because everything life would give my mother a few years after meeting my dad wasn't what she deserved. As they also say, "Life is what happens to you while you're busy making other plans." This afternoon, while my mom was making plans for her education, life was about to happen to her. A life that would later extend further to me.

She walked gently out of her parent's house after every family member had gone out when the man who would eventually become my father suddenly entered the compound. She was surprised to see him after all these months.

He walked up to her slowly as my mom's gaze was fixed upon him. As he got a few feet away from her presence, he let out the oddest words my mom had ever heard. "I went to Church with my girlfriend, whom I was thinking I would marry, but little did I know that I was wrong. Right in the Church, in the girl's presence, I was told she wasn't my wife, and that I should go fast and pray that my wife would appear in my dream.

Furthermore, the prophet told me that the time to get married had come. So, I did as he had told me. I prayed, fasted, and on the third day, I saw you in my dreams."

For some minutes, my mom stood there, confused and dumbfounded. She opened her mouth for words to fly out, but none came. The phrase 'the girl in my dreams' was supposed to be allegorical, but he wanted to make it literal. My mom was the girl in his dreams.

She couldn't believe her ears. He had tried to talk to her before, but she eschewed him. However, this was an eerie method of approach. Someone walks into your father's compound and tells you a prophet said you are his wife because you were in his dreams. If that were to be you, how would you have reacted? Would you have responded with a resounding no, a deafening scream, or sheer bewilderment? You can pause on what you think my mom's reaction was.

My mom was adamant at first. In fact, she was obstinate for long. However, after much disturbance, persuasion, and deliberation from him, she followed her newly found love to the prophet who had given the prophecy.

When they got to the prophet, he recalled the same thing he had told my dad in her presence. He roared with a voice as deep as a geyser. "I told him it was time for him to get married. So, I told him to make some prayers and whoever he saw in his dream was his wife, and it was you he saw."

The prophet's words were convincing, my father's persuasive, and my mother had fallen. My mom would sit comfortably on a wall of love, and she would suffer a terrible fall! Thankfully, she was strong and unbreakable.

Their courtship, they said, was fun and marked by an endearing tradition that spoke volumes about the depth of their connection. I wasn't born then, but these were the tales I was told. Tales I still find hard to believe were true.

… He never loved her as she deserved to be. Her love was deep, but his own wasn't. It was laced with deceit.

I was told every Christmas, they would emerge, dressed in coordinating attires, and he would always open the car door for her. They were always conspicuous and distinct, with matching yellow outfits that gave them out quickly and made them the cynosure of all eyes. All these happened at a time I reckon wasn't the norm, so it masked many issues.

You can forgive my mom for being carried away by love because she was young, innocent, and naïve. This was the first time she had such a feeling. As someone once said, "We accept the love we think we deserve." But that's the issue: he never loved her as she deserved. Her love was deep, but his' wasn't. It was laced with deceit.

Beneath the surface of their idyllic romance lay a revelation that added a bittersweet dimension to their love story. It was a truth known only to a select few—a truth that spoke of sacrifice, resilience, and unwavering commitment. My mother, with a hint of vulnerability in her voice, once confided in me that she had discovered she was pregnant with me before they exchanged vows. She had been blinded by love, and like a leaf on the surface of a stream, she went with the direction and strength of the flow.

One morning, she woke up, ran out of the room, and went to a corner of the house to throw up. Fantasy had taken her to bed, but reality woke her up. Alas! She was pregnant.

"No, no, no way. He and I have never spoken about pregnancy."

This is an extra about to be added to their love story. Some love stories are meant for just two people. When extra hands come in, they crumble.

"Wouldn't this news be too heavy to share or too big a burden for him to carry?" She mutters to nobody but herself and possibly to God.

It was a revelation that could have shattered the delicate illusion of their perfect romance because their love was still young and blooming. The Holy Book said, "Catch the foxes for us. Those little foxes before they ruin the vineyard of love, for the grapevines are blossoming!"

However, this little fox (pregnancy) didn't destroy their blooming vineyard. Instead, it deepened their bond, cementing their commitment to each other and the family they were destined to create. That pregnancy birthed me, and it catalysed their marriage. I wasn't there when they met, but I cemented their union.

Their marital journey wasn't all smooth sailing. When my dad's mother (the woman whom I would later love with all my heart) and her family came to ask for my mother's hands in marriage formally, they met minor challenges in the shape of my uncles, who initially refused to have my mother marry him. Why were they against it that much? Well, the reason or reasons weren't explicitly explained to me. But according to whispers, it was because my mom's brothers deemed my mom too young for marriage. Furthermore, they were all literate and wanted the same for my mom, who had become the family's lastborn after her junior brother's demise.

It took much beseeching and persuasion before the marriage finally happened. There's a maxim in my village that says, "What an elder can see while sitting, a child can't see it, even if he climbs a mountain."

My parents had always nurtured the dream of an extravagant wedding, but the pregnancy ensured they couldn't have that profligate dream come true…

I don't know if they saw a glimpse of the future my mom would face, but whatever they saw that made them say no at first, even if my mother had climbed the tallest mountain on earth, there was still no way she would have seen it.

My parents had always nurtured the desire for an extravagant wedding. However, the pregnancy ensured they couldn't have that profligate dream come true because, according to our culture and tradition, final marriage rites are not performed when a woman is pregnant, not until she delivers. However, my mom had to go to her husband's house to nurture her pregnancy. So, they allowed him to have her on the premise that traditional marital rites like the knocking on the door and four days of wine carrying for the parents, brothers, aunts, uncles, and other extended relatives had been done. So, traditionally, my mom had now become my dad's wife.

The girl was born

A few months after their marriage, I was born. The day I was brought into this world was lovely and exciting. The joy on the faces of everyone was unquantifiable. It was like sand on a beach. I was beautiful, shining, and metaphorically bouncing. You may ask how I knew since I was just a newborn. Well, at least I was there. Either as a newborn or not, you can't take my presence away from where I was born.

I wasn't the family's first grandchild, but my presence brought an elation similar to seeing an angel on earth. I was nicknamed the girl—a name that would become more renowned than my real name. It was what everyone called me, including my parents. Even the name rubbed off on my mom, and they would always call her Mummy the Girl or Sissy the Girl.

The way I was loved would make you question if something was hidden about my birth. My dad's sister had the first grandchild from my patrilineal side, but the child carried her father's name. So, I was the first grandchild to bear the family's name. Hence, I was welcomed into the world with an outpouring of love and adoration that knew no bounds. My grandmother, with her boundless affection and doting nature, treated me like the crown jewel of the family—a precious gift bestowed upon them by the heavens above. Her love was a source of comfort and joy, a constant reminder of the beauty and wonder that awaited me in this world, albeit tainted with moments of long-suffering and depression. Roland Leonhardt said, "Children bring us a piece of heaven on earth." I brought my parents their first piece of heaven on earth. However, even though my grandma had pieces of this heaven before me, the one I bought felt to her like the missing part of a puzzle. She was elated.

Looking back on those early years, I realise now the profound impact of my arrival on their lives. I was more than just a symbol of their love; I was a beacon of hope, a promise of a brighter future filled with endless possibilities, and the one who probably cemented their union. Maybe that's why they met my arrival with so much joy. They planted the seeds of love, and it grew into a tree. I was the first fruit it bore. So, they were happy when they saw it was good, especially when my other twin siblings, Marvin and Kevin, came along.

My dad had a Peugeot 505 car, which he used to carry my mum anywhere she wanted. I was told whenever he was driving, she would have her legs on the dashboard, enjoying the moment and her marriage, with their matching outfit, especially to a festival in our village during Christmas. Figuratively, they had the world at their feet and were having the fun of their life. They were young and beautiful, so why not?

My grandmother showered me with so much love. She seemed to have a special fondness for me. She assisted my mother to bathe me, feed me, and ensure everything I wanted then I got. She spoiled me so much, but thankfully, I was ripe, not rotten.

In retrospect, my parents' love story is not just a fleeting moment in time; it is a timeless saga of courage, resilience, and unwavering devotion. Their journey, marked by moments of joy and sorrow, triumph and adversity, left an indelible mark on my soul—a testament to the enduring strength of the human spirit and what it can achieve when faced with adversity. As I delve deeper into the annals of my family's history, I confront the complexities and challenges that shaped my parents' relationship. Behind the facade of a fairy-tale romance lay a narrative fraught with struggles, sacrifices, and the harsh realities of life.

I was there when it was sweet and sour, and like the title of Chinua Achebe's timeless classic book, I was there to see 'things fall apart.'

Despite the initial euphoria of their newfound love, my parent's marriage was not immune to the trials and tribulations that often accompany the journey of matrimony. I remember a few screams, little tears, and days when it all could have ended. I was there when it was sweet, sour, and non-existent. Like the title of Chinua Achebe's timeless classic book, I was there to see 'things fall apart.'

My dad was a hardworking and highly ambitious man. He loved working and accumulating money. However, he was always a little too dreamy and ambitious. These abstracts made him the man he was—the man my mother and us, the children, loved. These were the same abstracts that would turn him into the man he would later become.

He was an Oliver Twist, always wanting more. However, he worked tirelessly to ensure we never lacked the basic and good things of life whenever he was around. He was like the perfect husband and father.

He used to work in an oil rig, which made him very busy, and consequently, the job kept him away from us for days. While my dad worked, my mom would stay home to take care of us, grandma, and the house chores. Everything was going smoothly, everything was going fine, and everything was going our way. However, thankfully, my mom's love for education didn't wane in her moment of excitement. She decided to return to school so that having children wouldn't be her only life achievement. Thankfully, my dad agreed to it. She returned for her university entrance examination, known today as the Unified Tertiary Matriculation Examination (UTME). When the results were released, my mom's score was quite impressive. Consequently, she was admitted to the University of Port Harcourt.

For many months, everything was going according to my parents' plan. Even though my mom was now a student, my dad had no problem meeting all the family's needs. He was sufficient. However, the sufficiency never gratified him. His dreams were always larger than life. He always wanted more, but he wasn't wrong to do so. In the 2013 hit song, *'Am I Wrong'* by Nico and Vinz, they asked,

Am I wrong for thinking out the box from where I stay?
Am I wrong for saying that I'll choose another way? ...
... Am I wrong for trying to reach the things I can't see?

If I could answer Nico and Vinz, I would say no to all the questions above. You can't be wrong for wanting more or reaching for things beyond you. Dreams, hope, ambition, and the desire to be better than today are some of human's greatest motivators. However, what does reaching for new things make you do? Does it make you forget the ones you had and cherished? What do you give up to get the things you can't see? Do you give up the ones you see? What happens to the road that has brought you thus far when you choose another one? Do you ditch it and everything it represents for the new one?

I don't know your answers to my questions, but my father answered them. What answers did he give? Well, you are about to find out.

CHAPTER 2

FRAGRANCE AND FIRE

"Sometimes, beauty has to be agreed upon unanimously to be termed beautiful."

Sandra Mbeyi

They say beauty is in the eyes of the beholder. However, sometimes, you wonder how the beholder sees beauty in certain things. Is a butterfly beautiful? We would all unanimously agree with the assertion that it is. Is a rainbow beautiful? Yes, we can attest to the fact that it is. Is a Chimpanzee beautiful? I'll let you be the judge of that. So, sometimes, beauty must be unanimously agreed upon to be termed beautiful.

I was a beautiful child, and how I was treated was a sign that I was a product of love and was raised in it. However, I wasn't raised in the love my parents shared. Rather, I was raised in the love that others had for them, like my grandma, my parent's siblings, and the people around me. My grandma loved my dad so much, and it was this love she passed on to us, the grandkids.

As a child, everyone wanted to carry, play, and be friends with me. I was like the Queen of the neighbourhood kids because our family was renowned. They all wanted my grandma to bring me everywhere she visited. If my grandma had gone to the market without carrying me along, I felt she might have been sent back or gotten no discounted prices. I guess that's why she never went without me once. I was beloved by my community of Isiokpo in Rivers State, where we lived for years until my father's departure.

Travails

I was nothing but a child when my parents were young and married. However, I still vividly remember some of the events that happened, like it was a movie I watched before bed. Science has proven that, on average, the earliest memories that people can recall point back to when they were two-and-a-half years old. However, when I tell people I remember a few sketchy details about my parents when I was about five (another 2.5 years above the average retention age), they tend to always dismiss it by saying things like. "You were too young to know anything." "You were just a child." I wonder how they don't want to believe that I remember these things because, even then, I was deemed a bright kid.

I remember witnessing one of my parents' quarrels as a child. I was probably five at that time. Nonetheless, I remember one bright afternoon after returning from school, tired and thirsty. I saw my mom crying and complaining about something. At the same time, I stood in a corner of the house with a book in my hands. Mum was a reader, and she encouraged us to do the same.

I wanted to move closer to her to ask why she was in a deplorable state. I didn't know why she was crying hard; I just knew she was, and it didn't make me happy. However, I was too young to understand and ask why. As five-year-old children, crying over anything and everything was a routine in our lives. So, why should we question when others do it? However, even as children, we knew nobody would cry if they were happy. Crying is a sign that something is wrong, and you want it altered.

That day was the first time I'd seen my mother cry. It wasn't the best of sight for a five-year-old. I'm sure, even as an adult, you don't want to see that.

I remember walking up to her and trying to ask her what was wrong. My tiny hands rubbed slowly over her face to wipe her tears. I had watched some of my mates cry, and I wiped their faces for them; it is what kids do. However, wiping the tears off the faces of adults is something kids shouldn't have to do. My presence at that moment, or my hands rubbing against her cheeks, must have soothed her, or maybe she just didn't want me to see her like that, or my fingers had magic. One of these reasons stopped those tears from trickling down her eyes like heavy rain on a stormy night. That day was the first time I'd seen my mother cry. It wasn't the best of sight for a five-year-old. I'm sure, even as an adult, you don't want to see that.

Tragically, it wasn't even the last. Little did I know that it was the first of many to come. It was just the beginning, albeit a long hiatus before the next. Tragically, when next it came, even the magic in my hands wasn't enough to put a quick stop to it. It was like bursting a tank filled with water; it would be difficult to stop its flow. You just have to let it run out of water. Let it all out till there was nothing to let out anymore.

There's a song by a Nigerian gospel artist, Dunsin Oyekan, titled Fragrance to Fire, the chorus sings:

First, it was fragrance

Then it turned to fire …

Their love was fragrance at the beginning, beautiful to almost everyone who witnessed it. The matching outfits and visiting almost everywhere together were parts of the fragrance people perceived and believed was good, which made many envy their public show of love. It was a notion everyone held on to and passed along like an urban legend. They whispered it from one person's ear to another. Soon, the whispers became the noise that filled everyone's ears. Like a baton, they ran around with it, passing it on from one person to another and another.

Somewhere along the line, their love's fragrance stopped, and it became fire. I remember it because it burnt for a while, and we felt the heat. They would quarrel and quarrel for long hours. Why was that? I don't know because I was only a child. However, I know screams when I hear them, even if they emanate from their room faintly. The walls tried to stop it from getting to our room. Unfortunately, the walls had ears, my ears.

My grandma was very fond of me, extremely fond of me, because she loved me so much.

She thought I had reincarnated as her mom,
so she treated me specially...

We stayed in a semi-big house—a 5-bedroom apartment. There were four bedrooms inside the house and one in the backyard. In the middle of the compound was a small playground, and then we had a small local outdoor kitchen, which was the most used, even though we had a smaller indoor kitchen where we could put our cooker and pots. But we had our refrigerator there, and cooking happened in the outside kitchen. Then, there was my parents' room, and the room right next to theirs' was my uncle's, who was in the US then. The room was always locked when he was not around and only opened whenever he was in Nigeria. It was like a VIP room. We didn't enter unless he was around. We respected his absence as much as we did his presence. Also, there was my grandma's room, the room of the woman who played an immense role in my childhood.

Then, there was the living room and the dining room. Our room (my siblings and I) was directly opposite our parents' room, separated by a passage. Consequently, noises from their room got to ours before anyone else's. Sometimes, it even stops at our doorstep without going any further. I believe this is why many, apart from me, missed many of their minor conflicts—the walls obscured them. This is why not everyone had the same perspective I had of their marriage. The walls had concealed many things from many people.

Never look back

Everything has a limit it can't go beyond before breaking or spilling over. One evening, my mom would reach this limit or even surpass it. That day, a straw would break the camel's back. That straw would come on a cold evening. My siblings and I were playing in our compound as usual. I had probably developed better hearing sounds than everyone else because I could hear them going at each other with the highest decibel of noise their voices could produce. Albeit, it got to me faintly. It was like nobody else heard it apart from me.

Some minutes later, it stopped. However, just as I was about to return to whatever child's play I was actively participating in, my mom's voice came ringing down my ears from inside.

"The girl!"

I focused on ensuring I heard correctly because they never wanted us to be present whenever they yelled at each other. So, why is she calling me now? Furthermore, as I had said earlier, my nickname, 'the girl,' was more prominent than my real name. To some, it was a nickname; to some, it was a pet name; and to others, it was a way to praise me. However, in her fury, my mom would ditch the nickname she had always called me for my name. Anytime my mom called me my real name, I was either in trouble or being asked to stop what I was doing at once.

"Sandra!" She thundered to depict that this wasn't playtime.

I dropped the handful of sand I had taken and ran inside.

"Go and wear your clothes," she said angrily.

"Are we going somewhere?" I asked with my sonorous and innocent voice.

Her tone became high-pitched. "Go and change your clothes. We are leaving."

Haa! I exclaimed within. This woman isn't joking. I ran inside, quickly put something on, and returned to meet her.

I loved him so much, and I was afraid my mother and I were going somewhere to restart our lives without him. I didn't want to imagine that, but the reality was what was ahead as we took each step.

She carried Marvin on her back, Kevin on her left hand, and dragged me along with her right hand. Her face had become as rough as a pumice, and her look was as fierce as the blazing sun. There is a local Nigerian maxim that says, "Nobody dares point a torch in the lion's eyes without being a hunter." At that point, it felt real. She was the proverbial lion, and I wasn't a hunter, so I dared not ask her what was wrong.

We began to move farther away from the house, and within minutes, the house was out of sight. I kept looking back with almost every three steps we took. If I had been warned not to look back or risk being turned into a pillar of salt, I would have turned into it. However, I wasn't looking back out of disobedience; I was doing so out of the desire to see my dad coming after us. Strangely, he wasn't. I loved him so much, and I was afraid my mother and I were going somewhere to restart our lives without him. I didn't want to imagine that—a life without my dad.

Where is my dad, and why isn't he coming? Doesn't he know that they are taking his precious kids away from the house? Isn't he bothered that I was being taken away from him? I kept trying to devise a means to slow us down. Maybe he was running behind and would catch up with us shortly. I kept removing my hands from my mom's to fix my sandal, which was already laced perfectly, to make him catch up with us. If there was something I could do for us to be together, I would gladly do it.

However, my mom met each stop I took with a stern look. I didn't care; I just wanted my dad to catch up with us because I thought he was chasing me, his prized possession. Sadly, he wasn't.

Thankfully, that day, one of my dad's kin stopped my mom before we could go too far. My mum was angry, frantic, and with all her kids dressed up on a cold evening. This doesn't look like a family outing. Nobody goes to any family outing looking this fierce.

"Mama the girl, what's wrong? Where are you going with the kids at this time of the evening?" She asked with a voice lost between concern and surprise.

"Nothing." My mum responded sharply.

But her countenance betrayed her. Her face was telling everyone what her tongue tried to hide. All isn't well. I've come to learn as an adult that women can hide just about anything, but not when they are angry at the person they love.

"Mama the girl, obviously, there's something. Did you have a fight with your husband?"

My mom was silent for a few seconds. She didn't want to lie, and she didn't want to tell the truth.

Sometimes, in silence, there's guilt. Sometimes, there's a yes and other times, there's a no, but this is one of those times when silence meant a yes.

My dad's kin knew what her silence meant. But she felt that wasn't enough reason to leave her matrimonial home. "Hahan!" She exclaimed. "Is it because you had a fight with your husband that you are leaving your home? Where are you taking these children to at this time of the day? No, don't do that. Just go back home, please."

"No!" my mum insisted, "I have had enough!"

"Please, mama the girl, think about these children. Where do you want to take them? Where do you want to start from with three kids?"

Her words were a cliché, albeit highly convincing, making my mum want to change her mind and turn back. Still, I guess each time she imagined going back home, she tried to persuade herself that this wasn't the best option for her. She must have had enough of whatever my dad was serving her and wanted no more. So, she stood reluctantly, a sign to say no, I won't go back home.

I didn't want to leave home, I didn't want to leave grandma, and I didn't want to leave my

Like a country desperate to win a war but currently losing, my dad's kin brought out all the weapons in her armoury to convince my mom to return home. It must have been the last one she used on her that made her rethink the decision. I didn't know much about what was going on, but I was glad we met her on the road that day. I didn't want to leave home, I didn't want to leave grandma, and I didn't want to leave my friends. I had fallen in love with them, and I'm certain they had also fallen in love with me.

We turned back and headed home, but my father wasn't in sight as we walked closer. I thought I had heard footsteps, but I was wrong; it was just an imagination, a wish. It was all in my head. My little brain had concocted such a massive scenario. Realistically, he didn't come after us.

This was the first time we were torn apart as a family. Sadly, the next time we were was the last time we would ever be referred to as a family again. The day we separated was the end of the love that existed in our family. Today was nothing but a miniature sign of what's still to come.

CHAPTER 3

THE SEARCH FOR MORE

"Words have power and hold life, death, destruction, and rebuilding."

Sandra Mbeyi

When we got home, I felt lost between joy and gloom. The joy was because we were back home, which I loved the most, but the gloom was because we came back by ourselves.

My mum carried us back to our rooms and laid us down. My brothers slept, but my eyes were as bright as the midday sun. I watched as she walked back to her room to meet my dad. There was grave silence for a while, but then I could hear some rambling. Settling the issue or still deliberating on it, I couldn't figure out which it was exactly. My brothers had slept, oblivious to what was happening. But I was wide-eyed, with my ears picking sounds like radio waves.

Nonetheless, I was clueless about what was happening in their room but eager to know more about it, but that wasn't the time to enter their room. Whatever it was, I believe it wasn't for kids. In such scenarios, your parents' room becomes so sacred that only God should be in there with them at the time.

I wish dad hadn't travelled out to look for more...

Duty always calls

My dad did some jobs that I can recall vividly. He worked as an airport taxi for many years and did quite well. If my dad goes out a hundred times, he will bring back something for us a hundred and one times. Whenever he forgot to bring back something for us, we would all wonder if everything was right because it was unusual for that to happen. He did well as a father in how he provided for us, his children, and his wife.

If placed on a scale with unit one as poor and ten as rich, we would be on a five or somewhere between five and six. I wouldn't say we were rich, but we were far from being poor, far-flung from it. For a good reason, we avoided both extremes. However, our scales were slightly tilted towards the privileged. We were above average, and many families in the community looked up to us. Each time I look back, I wish dad hadn't travelled out to look for more. But who would ever blame any man for desiring more? Being ambitious is never a crime, but after he left and all the events that followed, it felt like it was. Everything came crumbling after—everything.

As an airport taximan, his duty was to pick people up from the international airport and ferry them to wherever they needed. For many, the destination was never within Rivers State; it was beyond. As a result, he spent a lot of his time on the road, especially outside Port Harcourt. I once told my mom that his job contributed to his ability to go a long time without seeing his family. Carrying passengers out of the state for days, especially at a time when the country was devoid of phones, computers, and the internet, prepped him to be able to stay without communicating with his family for long. Hence, by the time he travelled overseas, he was used to it—a life without his wife and children. However, to this day, my mum has never seconded this assertion.

Even though I loved his presence, I loved his return even more as he brought us gifts from almost every state he had ever driven into. If he travels to Kano, we get a gift synonymous with Kano. If he goes to Lagos, we get a gift synonymous with Lagos, and when he goes to the Eastern States, we get gifts that are synonymous with them. You can imagine how I felt when I heard he was travelling to America a few years later. Yes, you get my imagination right. Plenty of American gifts, right? But it wasn't going to be fated so. What I got from him as a child was as good as it got.

The beginning of love in our family tragically was its pinnacle. The happiness and joy we had as a family when I was a child was the best we ever had. If families had a mountain to climb to reach happiness, we began climbing from its peak. It looked like it would be clear sailing from that point, but it was a slippery slope that kept going moribund.

Words that began the destruction

Words have power and hold life, death, destruction, and rebuilding. History has documented men and women whose words changed the course of time. Some, like Martin Luther King Jnr and Nelson Mandela, whose words brought freedom. For some, like Rosa Parks and Malala of Maiwand, their words brought hope, courage, and victory, and for others, like St Telemachus and my dad, their words brought the destruction of something great.

Almost all the names mentioned above are familiar ones, barring three: Malala of Maiwand, St Telemachus, and my father. However, this book will teach you a lot about my father and family. But before I tell the tales of how my father's words brought about the end of a dynasty, I will briefly talk about the other two: Malala of Maiwand and St Telemachus.

Malala of Maiwand was the woman whose words, bravery, and sacrifice spurred the Afghans to their first-ever victory over the British at the second Anglo-Afghan War of 1880. When the Afghan soldiers were about to flee the battle in fear, she gave the famous speech that spurred them back to action and, ultimately, victory.

However, on the other hand, was St Telemachus, whose words led to the destruction of one of the world's greatest edifices, the Coliseum in Rome.

Telemachus was a fourth-century monk who lived in a monastery in Asia. He strongly desired to go to Rome and felt it was God's call to him. He took his possessions and headed for the capital. He arrived on a day the gladiators were to fight in the theatre, and everyone was heading to the arena to watch the spectacle. Telemachus walked into the arena and sat down among thousands of people who cheered as the gladiators came out to fight.

Immediately the battlers began to swing their weapons of death, the little monk got out of his seat, ran to the centre of the arena, and stood between two giant gladiators. Putting his hands up, he meekly cried, "In the name of Christ, stop!" The crowd scorned and jeered. One gladiator slapped Telemachus in the paunch with his sword, which made him fall to the ground.

Telemachus rose again and repeated his earlier statement, "In the name of Christ, stop!" This time, the crowd became angry that he was disturbing their joyous moments, so they chanted,

"Run him through!" A gladiator pierced through Telemachus' stomach with his sword. He fell into the dust, and the sand turned red as blood gushed out of him. Telemachus weakly cried out with the last energy he could muster, "In the name of Christ, stop." Then he died there on the Amphitheatre floor.

Within minutes, the whole arena became empty. That fight became the last gladiatorial contest in the history of the Roman Empire because three days after his death, the emperor ended the games by a decree.

They say the day he altered those words was the beginning of the Coliseum's end. I could imagine that because I know how simple words can alter family dynamics, life, history, and nature.

The day he said those words became the beginning of the end of our nuclear family.

The desire to sojourn

My father woke up one morning, seemingly lost in thought. Something was bothering him. My mom walked up to him slowly because it was an unusual sight for him to still be at home at that time of the morning. She creeps up slowly from behind. Her voice, albeit soft, was still enough to break the silence that had engulfed the room.

"Are you okay?" She mutters.

It was as if her words brought him back to life. He raised his head to look at her. However, he uttered no word in return.

"Is everything okay?" She muttered again.

"I want to leave Nigeria."

My mum looked around to be sure he was the one who spoke and to be certain he was talking to her. Having confirmed that it was just the two of them present, she turned to him and said, "You say?"

"I want to travel out of the country."

My mum rushed toward him. "You want to leave the country, why?" At first, she couldn't fathom where the idea came from because they had spoken about it some years ago, just a few months after I was born, which she refused because she felt it wasn't a good idea. He had never brought it up until that day, of which he had no reason to.

"I want to go and make a better life for us."

"A better life for us," she bellows, "But we are doing well enough. We are almost like the envy of the whole village. What else do you want?"

"I want to give my children more." He responded. "If, with God and my effort, we can do this, imagine what would happen if I travelled abroad."

At the time, my uncle (dad's junior brother) was in America. He would visit Nigeria at various times, dwelling in our house throughout his stay. He lived affluently and said great things about his country of sojourn. He must have sold my dad an outlandish dream in one of his tattletales.

Whenever my uncle was around, I loved listening to his pleasant tales about the United States, especially when he talked about the buildings, roads, and transportation system. His words were beautiful, and he presented the country as a paradise. Maybe my father was infected with the possibility of a beautiful, pleasant dream there. Who knows, maybe my dad would have dreams of being in the USA whenever he slept. So, he decided to make the dream a reality.

It was a dream at first, only to become a nightmare at the end.

He sold this dream to my mom, and in less than a heartbeat, she accepted his proposition of travelling to the United States to make a better life for his family. He was family-oriented when he was here with us, so why not? He never gave anyone any reason to doubt him, so there was no need to. Perhaps my mother imagined the dream he sold to her, too. He must have promised to accomplish prodigious things for the family when he arrived, and then he would come back to pick us all within a short time of travelling. Those dreams must have been beautiful. If only my mum knew the dream would cost her the love, touch, and protection of a husband, she would have stood against it. It was a dream at first, only to become a nightmare at the end.

CHAPTER 4

THE NEW BEGINNING

"People always mistake change for progress, but not all changes are progressive. Some are nothing but disaster."

Sandra Mbeyi

Sometimes in 1932, Protestant theologian Reinhold Niebuhr composed one of the greatest short prayers that ever existed. It was called the Serenity Prayer, and it reads.

Oh, God, give us the courage to change what must be altered,

The serenity to accept what cannot be changed,

And the insight to know the one from the other.

It is a prayer millions of people have said since it was first composed. However, what happens, or what do we do when confronted with things we can't accept and, simultaneously, can't change? What gives? What goes? If unstoppable meets immovable, what happens? A reality must be altered. Something must change; something must give. It's either unstoppable stops or immovable moves.

My mom and I were at certain points when confronted with this dilemma. A situation we couldn't accept, yet it stood as one we couldn't change.

My dad had shared the story of his impending departure with my mom, but there was another important person he had yet to share it with. Who was that person? It was his mother, my grandma. He knew he had no other choice than to share it with her. So, he walked into her room to share the exciting news. At first, she was elated. The news was galvanising. She already had a son in the United States, and now the other is about to join. She was excited, and that was putting it mildly. However, like opium, the thrill wore out almost as quickly as it had engulfed her. She was amenable at first, but it didn't seem the best decision on second thought. Both her sons are about to leave her.

Consequently, her subsequent reaction was devastation. She had only two sons, and she was about to lose them to the cold regions of the United States. Her countenance became dour, and her soul troubled within her. My grandma would soon prove excellent at hiding secrets, but today, she couldn't conceal this emotion. It was as conspicuous as the rising sun.

My mom waded in. Little did she know that her words would be the one to undo her marriage.

"Are you okay, aunty?" My dad asked with a voice as troubled as waters on a stormy night. However, she wasn't okay because his words weren't euphonious.

"This your news of wanting to travel to America?" She responds with a voice opposite to his.

"Isn't it good news?" He questions softly.

"Yes, it is. But..."

"There's nothing to be afraid of or panic about, aunty. I'm going there to make more money. I have spoken with my brother, who has advised me to come. Look at what I've achieved here. Imagine what I will achieve when I am there."

"Exactly, look at what you've achieved here. I believe you can achieve even more." My grandma retorts.

They were at each other's throats for some minutes while my mom watched, hoping they would reach a consensus. However, seeing there was no headway, my mom waded in. Little did she know that her words would undo her marriage perpetually.

"Aunty," she mutters softly.

My grandma was called aunty by my dad and his siblings because when her brother lost his wife, they raised his kids together. Her brothers' children, who were older than hers' called her aunty because she was their aunt. When her kids were born, they naturally followed their cousins to call her aunty and the name stuck. Everyone began calling her aunty, including us, the grandkids, and everyone who knew her.

"I trust that he will go there and make us all proud. Even now that he is here, you can see how hardworking he is. I believe when he gets there, he might get a better job than this and even send a lot of money home."

"I don't fancy this idea of travelling when he is already doing well here. But if you say so, what else can I say?"

My dad cuts in. "Aunty, I know it won't be easy to have both sons in a country far away from you. I know how you feel, but once I get there and sort myself out, I will visit timely. I have spoken with my brother, who has assured me of a place to stay and promised me a place to work. I know you don't want to be alone, but my wife and children will remain with you. You will still have your beloved grandchildren to always play with. Family surrounds you."

A storm had brewed in my grandma, but somehow, my dad had found a way to still it. There was calm; there was peace, and there was love, but only for a while. From here, everything was only about to go moribund.

Aunt's warnings

The news of my dad's impending travel kept snowballing, and it soon reached the doorsteps of my mom's elder sister. However, she didn't take the news lying down. She was a frequent traveller overseas and had lived in the United Kingdom for a while. She had just returned from one of her numerous trips a few weeks before the news broke.

My aunt's words stood as a warning, but if only my mom had listened to them, maybe things might have panned out differently, or were those happenings just inevitable? Well, we will never know.

"Your marriage is too young for this. You've only been married for less than six years. Your children are little. Your first daughter is just five; she barely knows much, and you still have two other little children. This is when you need him here the most, not in a faraway land. Also, you are a student with an education to pursue. I have travelled out of this country several times and I know how it is abroad. Your marriage is simply too young for this. My sister, you all need him here. His children, you, and everyone; you all need him now!"

Even if her words were true, there wasn't much my mom could do. My dad had decided, and nothing would stop him from pursuing this quest.

Coming to America

The preparations for my dad's travel to the USA began. The few days before he left were some of our happiest as a family and the best we would ever have as one. Everything was beautiful. The way he treated us, my mom, grandma, and everyone else around us at the time.

The news of my father travelling to America made me excited that everything was about to change. Yes, everything did change, but there's a misconception about the word 'change.' People always mistake change for progress, but not all changes are progressive. Some are nothing but disaster. Like my father's journey would be on the family and my mental health—a colossal disaster.

A few days before his departure, my effervescent dad spoke with infectious energy and brought hope to everyone his departure would affect.

When the long-awaited day for his travel came, we went to the airport in our dad's car. I can't remember who drove us, but we all went as one big happy family. He hugged us all, but as he tried to hug my brother, Marvin, he shrugged his shoulder, denying him the opportunity for a final hug. Marvin was two then, and we believed he didn't know what he was doing. However, my dad didn't see it that way because, years later, he referenced that incident.

Lastly, he hugged my mom, and she waved her ultimate goodbye gleefully. Tragically, it became the last passionate goodbye they would ever have.

Days and weeks passed since my father left, and not a word from him or his brother whom he had gone to meet.

Days and weeks passed after my dad left, and not a word came from him or his brother, whom he had gone to meet. Finally, they were both able to communicate, but my dad had encountered severe immigration challenges. He needed some papers to complete his process, which would enable him to get a stay in the country. Immediately, my mom swung into action. Thanks to her never-say-die attitude, she was able to get everything he needed. Finally, he was granted entry into the United States.

The ties that bind

My mum's hands were full. Managing the home and three little children, plus taking care of my dad's mother, whose health was failing, and still having to go to school to learn, was a demanding life to live.

Anytime my mom wanted to communicate with my dad, she would have to go to the main city to make calls from a phone booth or plan a date and time at his friend's house in the town. Occasionally, I would go with her to speak with him. Sometimes, she would go with other members of the family who wanted to talk to him. Other times, whenever she returned from school in the evening, she would branch at a phone booth to make the calls. As a result, communication between them wasn't smooth sailing. They had to plan the dates and times when they wanted to communicate.

Furthermore, when someone comes from America to the village, those abroad will send letters, videotapes, and gifts through that person to the family members. Also, when that person was returning, everyone in the village who had families abroad would return the same gesture. Whoever came to Nigeria or travelled to the USA was the means of communicating and passing messages. My father would send videos of him, telling us how the USA was. However, amidst these difficulties, they tried to ensure they regularly heard each other's voices.

Communication between them was one challenge they had to deal with. However, a bigger one was about to surface. In a little while, my grandma's health began to deteriorate. Her energy began to sap, and she could barely do anything herself. My mom would always take her for monthly check-ups and prepare her special meals because she had diabetes. It was one of the first down points of my childhood. My grandma was one of the first best friends I had. Consequently, seeing her in pain broke my little heart. I loved her as I will always.

Thankfully, my mom did her best to keep the smile on her face. It was beautiful. However, my grandma would play one of the most villainous roles in my mom's life in a few weeks. To echo the words of Sheldon's mum in the series Young Sheldon, "Some are better grandmas than moms." However, I would say some are better grandmas than mothers-in-law.

A few years after my dad left, everything seemed to be going fine, but it would all blow to pieces one gloomy day when my mom stopped by the phone booth to make her usual calls to my dad. That day, everyone's lives would come crashing down.

At times, when she left the village for the city to receive lectures in school, she would visit a phone booth to speak with my dad. That day was one of those days, but the outcome was nothing like the previous days. They say change is life's only constant, and it was about to apply to my mom. Everything was about to change.

She excitedly called my dad's phone, but it dissipated when the call was picked up at the other end. She came with immense joy, but she would leave with none.

The person at the other end picked up and said hello. She was expecting her husband's voice, but surprisingly, a woman had picked. My mom was silent for a few seconds. Before my dad left, many people tried to warn my mom about why she shouldn't allow him to travel for their marriage's sake and the possibility of a strange woman entering the picture. Instantly, the fear of those warnings coming to pass engulfed her for a while, but she shook it off. My mom asked the woman who she was, and her biggest fears would come to pass. The woman introduced himself as his wife, and my mom heartbreakingly introduced herself as my dad's sister. To compound her woes, the woman mentioned my dad's sister's name, which meant she knew my dad's family, and they must have had several conversations. My mom's marriage was falling apart, and she was the last to know about it.

No matter how bad you think this is, the worst is yet to come. The woman continued the conversation with my mom, but unable to listen or bear the heat, my mom finally told the lady she was my dad's wife, and they had three children together in Nigeria. The woman at the other end was puzzled, and it was palpable in her silence. However, she broke the silence with the most demeaning words my mom could have heard. "He told me he had three children with a woman in Nigeria. However, he told me the woman is his mom's househelp, and they were never married."

In that instant, my mom dropped the phone and walked home, oblivious to what was happening around her. She was lost, broken, forlorn, and shattered. You could forcefully throw a piece of glass on the floor, and it wouldn't crumble into as many pieces as my mom's heart.

She needed a pillar of support and someone to share this with because it was too much to bear. In physics, there's a heat transfer process called conduction. In this method, when a part of a material takes too much heat, it spreads it to its other parts to help its absorption. My mom had taken too much heat and needed to share it with someone else. She couldn't share it with us—the kids—because we couldn't have withstood such heat; it was beyond us. So, she proceeded to meet someone who could empathise with her. She went to my grandma to explain everything that had transpired amidst tears and hurt. But my grandma refused to conduct a part of her heat. After she was done explaining everything, my grandma responded most devastatingly.

"Why did you have to tell the woman you are his wife? Don't you know you are putting him in danger? Do you want the woman to be angry and kill my son?"

My mom was devastated. She couldn't believe her ears. It was nowhere near anything she had envisaged. She was expecting sympathy, love, and apologies but got none. Which do you think is worse? To be betrayed by someone you love or to be abandoned by those you've served? I'll let you be the judge of that. However, as I said earlier, "Some are better grandmas than mothers-in-law."

CHAPTER 5

THE REVELATION

"The irony of life is that humans don't control life; it's controlled by time, and time never waits for anyone."

Sandra Mbeyi

For my mom, what had transpired on the phone that day had turned her day into night. For weeks, she was desolate, lonely, and disgruntled. The world underneath her feet was quaking. Everything was falling apart, but she had to hold on to life and live for her children's sake. She was hanging by a thread. But she shared none of her predicament with us—her children. I didn't know about all this until years later. I didn't know why she kept all this vital and heartbreaking information from us. Well, maybe because it was heartbreaking, and she didn't want the knowledge of the happenings to affect other areas of our lives. So, she wanted to absorb them all. Unfortunately, years later, I was in her shoes and did the same thing: facing it alone.

The Holy Book said in **Ecclesiastes 4:9-11**, "Two are better than one because they have a good return for their labour: If either of them falls, one can help the other up. But pity anyone who falls and has no one to help them up." My mum fell badly. She fell and was hurt, but the tragedy is that she had nobody to help her up. She didn't want to tell her mother and siblings what her husband had done because it would negatively impact their relationship and their perception of him. She didn't want to tell us, the kids, because she didn't want to villainise our dad. Yet, the people she told didn't have any care in the world. At that point, she knew only she could bring herself out of this valley. Thankfully, my mom had always made God's word her watchword, even in the days of her youth. With God's word and prayer, she pulled herself out of the abyss life had plunged her.

After weeks of being down and out, she picked herself up and began attending lectures back in school. She was all we had at the time, and even though she didn't tell us about her predicament, her gloom began to reflect around the house. Surreptitiously, our school results began to mirror the state of our family. When we brought home that term's results, my brothers had fallen off badly. Their results were as bad as rotten eggs.

My mom was worried. She knew her state of mind was becoming evident in her children's results. Thus, she concluded there were two things left to do: heal her mind and change our school to a much better one.

My mom was the kind that never joked with education, either hers or her children.

Micah 7:8 says, "Do not gloat over me, my enemies! For though I fall, I will rise again. Though I sit in darkness, the LORD will be my light." My mom had to rise again quickly for her children's sake. It was like she had been sitting deliberately in darkness and now needed to step into the Saviour's light. Her children shouldn't crumble with her even if she was crumbling within. This is not their burden to bear. So, she decided to rise.

My mom called my dad for the first time since the incident, explaining that she needed to change our school from Isiokpo to Port Harcourt. She knew she had to do the self-healing without anyone's help, but changing our school was something she couldn't do all by herself. However, immediately she told my dad about the plan to change our school from the village to a better one in Port Harcourt city, he vehemently said no. His reasons were that he didn't have any money and he didn't want us to leave the village home. His reaction was stolid. However, my mom wouldn't bulge. She knew this was about our life, future, and foundation. If the foundation of our education is destroyed, what would we be able to do in the future? My mom was the kind that never joked with education, either hers or her children. I took that from her and will forever bear my gratitude for it.

Even though she wanted the best for us, she couldn't decide alone. So, she consulted my grandma (my dad's mum). She explained how our grades had declined and the need for a change. I would repeat this, as I've said many times. "Some are better grandmas than mother-in-law." As long as it was for her grandchildren to have a better life, my grandma was ready to go miles. She agreed and supported my mom in moving us to the city to have an opportunity for a better education.

These were the first days of my mom's gloom. Her husband was no longer hers, and her children's results had plunged. People say after the storm comes the sun, and after the night comes the day. But it seems, for my mom, after the night comes another night, and after the storm, more thunder and lightning are lurking. However, she would turn her night into day with God's help, prayers, and determination.

My mom changed our school and got us lesson teachers. Within a short time, there was significant progress in our results. Furthermore, my mom graduated from the University with one of her department's best performances.

Things were looking rosy again, and it seemed like she had picked up the pieces of her life. People have always argued that after the night comes the day, and after the storm comes calm, but what comes after the day? Or will it be light forever? What comes after the sun? Or will it be sunny forever?

Tragedy was about to strike again as my grandma's health became worse than ever. This time around, she suffered a stroke and needed more care and attention than ever before. With almost none of her children nearby, my mom was the last resort. Thankfully, she ensured grandma got all the care and attention she needed. Most of the time, she would be on admission at the hospital, yet my mom would stay there with her until she was discharged.

When my dad heard of his mother's predicament, he wanted to visit Nigeria but couldn't because he hadn't gotten the necessary travel documents. Consequently, there was only one thing left to do: call my mom and plead with her to help attend to his mom. Even though my mom hadn't heard from him in a while, she wasn't hesitant to heed his plea to help care for his mom.

Sadly, my grandma passed away. It was a sad day for me because she was someone I had grown to love. One of the people I loved as a child was no longer with us.

Once again, my dad needed my mom. So, he called her to make one more request. He told her to help him ensure his mom gets a befitting burial. He wanted her to work hand in hand with his brother (my uncle). Again, my mom agreed to do that which he desired. As far as she was concerned, he was still her husband, and we were still his children.

My mom played an immense role in grandma's burial. However, something uncanny would happen. When the burial flyers were printed, my mom noticed something unusual. My grandma was said to be survived by her children and grandchildren. However, there was an odd name when the grandchildren's names were listed. One that my mom couldn't recognise. He was my half-brother. Yet, none of us knew he existed until that very day.

My mom was still hoping and fighting for her marriage. Maybe, one day, her husband would come to her to apologise for all the pain he had caused and go back to being a loving husband and father. This is what my mom had hoped. But it appeared at that point that the hope was dashed. This is the end of the road. My mom had just healed from the first heartbreak he caused. He has done it again. Her tears had dried, but it seemed her pillow was about to be damp again.

My mom was distraught, devastated, angry, and sad. All the undesirable emotions engulfed her all at once. However, she took it all in good faith.

A few weeks after the burial, the news of the immense role my mom played got to him at lightning speed. He called her. But, if you think he called her to say thank you, then think again because, like my mom, you are about to be disappointed.

She picked up his call to listen to what he had to say. She was expecting one or both of two things: a thank you or an apology. Disappointingly, she got none.

"Hello. I have heard so much about you from my younger brother. So, I'm calling to tell you that, henceforth, our ties are severed. You are free to go your way as I have gone mine. You and I are no longer a couple."

I could have sworn her heart had healed, and her wound had closed, but that very day, he tore everything to pieces once again. He was strumming her pain with his words, and each time her heart had healed, he would try to hurt it again.

The last time my mom's heart was broken over the phone, she waited for the call to end before she broke down in tears. But this time around, she couldn't be that strong. She couldn't hold her tears. She responded in a soft, teary voice, "Is this the thanks I get for caring for your mother? Is this the thanks for changing her adult diapers, washing, and feeding her? Is this what I deserve?" Tears trickle down her eyes like heavy rain on a stormy night. It was like the pain was happening all over again. Her wound was healing, but he reopened it and left it to bleed. She was just coming out of the darkness, climbing out of the abyss, and beginning to get things back on track, but he broke it again. Life shouldn't be this cruel.

Without a speck of emotion, he roars, "Have you heard me?" Then he cuts the call on her.

Sometimes, you feel like all your trouble is over, but when everything feels like it's coming back to life, it crumbles again. I guess that's why they call it the rise and fall.

I learned many things subconsciously from my mom. However, the two most important were God and her excessive thirst for knowledge. They were her watchword and solution to almost everything, and she ensured we abided by it.

Once again, my mom, with no other choice, had to pick up her broken self. While this was going on, she never complained to us or told us anything about our dad's misdemeanours and never once sat us down to slander him. An admirable trait, but I wish she had told me everything before the years we all travelled to meet him in the USA. He showed my mom hell and would show me the lake of fire.

However, before I get to that part, it was my final year in high school, and I was to sit for my final secondary school exams (SSCE/WAEC). However, I noticed my mom didn't register me on time. I reckoned my dad hadn't sent money. He used to send money monthly, but somehow, he stopped. We didn't know why, but we would later find out he didn't have a job.

The deadline drew closer, but my name wasn't a part of those to sit for the exams. My mom had a job then, but unfortunately, it didn't pay much.

My mom visited my school on our visiting day and discussed paying for my exam registrations. I didn't know why it was difficult for my exam fees to be paid, so I told her to call my dad, but she was reluctant to make the call. However, after much persuasion, she did. When she told him I was in my final year at high school and needed money for my exams, my dad responded quickly. "I don't have any money."

My mom couldn't believe her ears. "You mean you don't have money for your daughter's exam registration?"

"Yes," he replied before ending the call.

My mom was livid, and that's putting it mildly. She decided to call and complain to my dad's younger brother about how my dad neglected his children's examination fees. If you think my dad's response was the worst, then you are about to hear something even more sinister.

The irony of life is that humans don't control life; it's controlled by time, and time never waits for anyone.

When called, he responded, "If my brother said he doesn't have money, then he doesn't have. Will you kill him?"

At that point, my mom saw no light at the end of that tunnel. She knew she had to find another way because the person whose responsibility it was had denied it.

The irony of life is that humans don't control life; it's controlled by time, and time never waits for anyone. What is ahead doesn't matter; time will ferry you to it. Little by little, time was ferrying me to my examination's registration deadline. Thankfully, my mom was able to rally around for the money, and just days before the final deadline, she paid in full.

Sadly, the WAEC result of everyone in my school was withheld. It took my mom a lot to raise the money; devastatingly, that effort didn't count. It was one of the first gloomy moments of my life. However, I didn't allow it to be an anchor, which kept me from sailing.

Within a short time, my dad and the woman separated. However, if you think this made him reconsider his relationship with my mum, you have gotten it wrong. Instead, my dad had associations with other women.

Like a bird, time flew. Like the wind, time passed by, albeit unseen. The tempest my dad had brewed a few years ago had calmed. It wasn't easy to bring calmness to it, but somehow, my mom did it with God's help.

With his words

Sara Teasdale said, "It is strange how often a heart must be broken before the years can make it wise." Sometime in 2006, my dad would break my heart for the first time—the first of many—and only the years made it better, albeit many years.

Heartbreaks come in many forms and from different people. However, mine came from my dad when he visited Nigeria in 2006 for the first time since his departure.

I lost two things the day my dad came to see me in Nigeria for the first time. I lost my innocence and my happiness.

A day before my dad visited Nigeria, I called and told him I was sick and needed some money for my treatment. I can't remember his exact words, but he didn't send any. Unknown to me that he would be on his way to Nigeria immediately after our phone conversation. Sadly, he never said a word about it to my mom, siblings or me.

I was at home with my mom in our Rumuokoro apartment in Port Harcourt, the Rivers State capital, while my brothers were in boarding school.

That morning, there was a knock on the door, and when I opened it, I found out it was my cousin. He was my dad's elder sister's son and had never visited us until that very day. Maybe he had, but I don't remember. He entered, and my mom greeted him. I hugged him, and he sat close to me. My mom offered him food, but he declined the offer. He talked and joked with us for a little while. However, within a short period, he said he was leaving and asked if I could see him off. I was not properly dressed since I was just sitting at home when he came. As I proceeded to see him off to within a few metres from the house, my mom beckoned on me to change into something different, so I did. I walked him out to the street and saw the biggest shock of my life. My dad, whom nobody had seen in years, was standing by a blue SUV, which I recognised as his younger sister's.

I glanced at my cousin, gazed at the car again, and thought to myself. 'Our dad had arrived in Nigeria and we, his children, were the last to know.' All his extended family members knew of his arrival before his children. That was a glimpse of the level of importance and love our dad showed us.

Immediately he saw me, he said, "The girl, it's I, your daddy."

I didn't know whether to be excited or sad. What sort of surprise is this? Is this even real? Is this my dad? Seeing each other for the first time in years was supposed to be a day filled with love, joy, and emotion. Tragically, it was a day devoid of all.

He told me to get in the car, but I told him no because my mom would be worried. I was only supposed to be gone for a few seconds. He said he would call her, and I insisted before entering the car. He called my mom, and the phone rang.

My mom picked up and said, "Hello."

He responded with a voice devoid of emotion to a woman he hadn't seen or spoken to in years. "Chinedu, it's Achi. I have the girl with me. Do you have any issues with that?"

My mom was in shock. She couldn't believe her ears. Her husband, who hadn't seen her in years and whom they departed with so much love and affection, was a few metres away from her door, but he chose not to see her. He was close to her but opted to remain far away.

I believe her heart must have skipped a beat or maybe even two because there was a sudden pause from her end. She was devastated and sad. Honestly, I would be if I were her. Nonetheless, she summoned the composure to tell him she was okay with his proposition. So, he took me back to his hotel room. As we drove to the hotel, I didn't know what to think or say because we barely spoke. My dad had returned after many years, and we were like strangers with little to talk about. The man meant to teach me love taught me heartbreak instead.

We went to the hotel, and there, his friend kept bringing him prostitutes. I don't know which was worse to witness: seeing your mother being abandoned or watching your father philandering with coquettish women, even knowing his daughter was watching. I remember one of the women. Her name was Anita, and I formed a bond with her and collected her number at some point.

I didn't know my dad had a problem with my mum. She ensured we had no idea what he had been doing to her, but he would use his mouth to unravel the secret that day. He called my mom all kinds of names and told me he didn't care if I knew nothing. He said the marriage was over, and he hated her. I was shattered as I listened to my dad utter those words about my mom.

We visited my brothers in school, but they didn't let him see them because he was not registered.

Martin Luther King Jr. said, "In the end, we will remember not the words of our enemies, but the silence of our friends." How about if our enemies were silent and our friends were the ones speaking badly about us, saying the kind of things my father said about my mom? We can never forget that, too, right? A local maxim says, "When you want a deaf man to hear what you have to say, pass the message to his children." He wanted to tell her these things but didn't want to see her, so he passed the message to me.

We visited my brothers in school, but they didn't let him see them because he was not registered. We had to call my mom, who permitted him to see them. She didn't deny him that privilege, even after everything he had said and done. When they called my brothers out, they asked me who this man was, and I said he was their father. They didn't know him because they were toddlers the last time they saw him.

A few days later, my brothers vacated from school, and we went to pick them up. My mom was also there to pick them up, but someone had lied to my dad that if he saw my mom, he would die. So, on sighting her, he yelled dramatically at the driver to drive away. It was all uncanny, but he brought my brothers home with my mom's permission. He then proceeded to break their little hearts, too. I wanted to protect them so badly from what he had done to my heart, but I couldn't. He filled them with unkind and vile words about our mom. I watched as my brother cried so badly in the back of that SUV. An image that haunts me to this very day.

When I returned home from the hotel, I met my mom sitting on the floor with her sisters, mom, and aunts, weeping profusely. It was as if someone had died.

I asked her why she didn't tell me what had been happening all this while. Her eyes were filled with pain, pity, and anguish. She told me she wanted to preserve my innocence and peace. I told her I would have preferred to have heard it from her than in the manner my dad just did. While we were still on that subject matter, she told me I had to jump on a bus to Isiokpo to give him the key to his house in the village because he was there and about to break the door. When I got to Isiokpo, I met him, his uncle with his wife, and a prophet.

They said my mom hid dollars in the drawer and did some diabolical things. This prophet prayed with him and my uncle and aunt while I stared at them. That was the tale all through his stay in Nigeria. He said and did so many inimical things that I remember crying and begging him at a point to stop, but he didn't.

The visa

My parents' last conversation was that whenever our visas were ready, he would call to take us abroad. Finally, they were ready, and strangely, mine was included, even though he had told me to my face when he was in Nigeria that it wouldn't. Tragically, when the visas came out, our mom's own was missing. He had sworn not to include hers and even told her he had cancelled the papers he had used to file for her. We didn't think it was a joke, but we didn't think he would see it through.

Naturally, your dad inviting you to the United States ought to be a thing of joy for you and your mom, but it was the opposite, especially seeing that our support and pillar of strength—our mom—wouldn't be going with us.

Even though my mom knew travelling to the United States would significantly boost our careers and education, she feared what our dad could do to us when she was no longer in the picture. Besides, we were now the only thing she had besides her first university degree. So, she sought advice from people. However, many of them didn't know what her predicament had been. They judged by the news they heard, not the circumstances surrounding it. Maybe if they had known differently, they would have advised differently.

Most of those she told were all excited at the news. Your children are going to the US to meet their father. Should this still be up for debate? Your answer should have been an instant yes. They advised her to let us travel abroad, listing all the benefits involved. However, they didn't know the intricacies.

For days, my mom would sit lonely, contemplating and weighing the possible outcomes of the decision she was about to make. On the one hand, she was a woman who didn't have a good job and enough money to comfortably send her children to school. So, she feared our education might come to an abrupt end. On the other hand, it was a chance to travel to a great country and be availed of a world-class education and a chance of a better future. The choice was supposed to be simple, but it wasn't. But she finally chose the possibility of having a better education and future with our father. However, that road was thorn-filled, and it bruised my siblings and me emotionally, psychologically, and mentally.

From that day, my mom resorted to serious prayer sessions. She was unsure of what we were going to the United States to face, and she feared it.

After my mom concluded that she would allow us to travel to the United States, I remember her calling us all together one morning to inform us about our trip. We were not as excited as kids travelling to the United States should be. My mom convinced and advised us not to be weary and gloomy.

Knowing we were going without her, we asked if there was any chance she would be joining us within a short while. She smiled faintly. Each time I look back and remember that smile, with the knowledge I would later have, I know that it came from a place of pain and regret. With that faint, painful smile, she muttered, "No, my children, I won't be with you soon. But I promise I will come to you sometime in the future."

Our emotions became checkered. We were lost between fear and heartbreak because we didn't want to go without our mom.

From that day, my mom resorted to serious prayer sessions. She was unsure of what we were going to the United States to face, and she feared it. So, before we left, she sent her prayers ahead of us to clear our path and make crooked ways straight.

A few days before we left, she prayed fervently and anointed us. She declared that as long as our two feet touch the United States of America's soil, we shall succeed in all we endeavoured. She prayed and prayed from the depths of her heart.

Finally, the long-awaited day came. We were dressed and ready to go. As we left, my mother hugged and bade us farewell with tears and prayers.

Our plane finally left. We were now far from Nigeria and getting close to the United States. We were excited, but little did we know we were about to shake hands with the gates of hell.

CHAPTER 6

A NEW FOUNDATION

"One bad thing about dreams is that they all don't come true."

Sandra Mbeyi

They say everything that goes up must come down. They call it the law of gravity. Our plane went up in Nigeria and came down in the United States. I had a gust of mixed emotions, lost between fear and excitement.

The fear came from the fact that I would be doing life without my mom. An action I had never pulled before. There was rarely a day I didn't see her, but now I am about to go an unknown amount of time without her.

However, the excitement came from two reasons. It was the first time I was entering a plane and travelling out of the country, and second, because of the prospect of the beauty the future holds, like him sending for my mom to join us in the US within a short time. Maybe this is the point where everything changes. This is the transformation we've all been waiting for.

Even while we were wide awake on the plane, we dreamt! We dreamt of how beautiful America would look, the good life that awaited us, the excitement we would see on our dad's face, and the beautiful things he might do trying to make up for the lost years. But one bad thing about dreams is that they all don't come true. However, feel free to have them because having them doesn't cost you anything; achieving them can cost everything.

My parents may have been separated for many years, but nothing could separate me from the love I had for my dad. Even though I saw him a few years ago, and he said unscrupulous things about my mom, I loved him like I did from the beginning—nothing less. I was angry at him, but anger and hate aren't on the same pedestal.

Even my brothers would call me daddy's girl because of my love for him. However, as they say, change is inevitable, but we were too young to know. My siblings and I were moving mindlessly into a trap. My dad's trap. Our coming was like a game to him, but thankfully, he never won.

My dad's love for us had changed, and it had waned. However, we didn't know.

Finally, we landed. When we did, it was like we were holding hands with paradise. We were cleared from the airport, and my dad came to pick us up to take us to his home. I can list some of the happiest days of my life, and that day would be amongst the top three. However, my dad's actions would ensure I would rue that day for long.

We got to his house at Little Moon Trail Street, Rock Springs, Wyoming. When we entered, he showed me my room. That was the first time I had a room to myself. Back home in Nigeria, I had always shared rooms, but here comes freedom. It appears my first night was beginning to pan out like I had dreamt. Someone, please, call the heavens! Dreams do come true!! We went to get some foodstuff, and he tried to get to know us. We've missed many years of each other's lives, so there was much to know and talk about.

I noticed the woman living with him and tried to figure out who she was. Well, I found out that she was his new Kenyan girlfriend.

As days passed, people in the city began coming to tell us different things. Some had good things to say, and some had terrible ones to say. Some said they were sorry for us because we came without our mother, especially since we looked young and innocent. It was scary having people sympathising with us. It was almost as if they could see, and had seen, certain things we should be worried about. But this is my father's house, and I shouldn't be living in fear of what he can do to me.

Living in a house with another woman who wasn't my mother was odd. Watching them laugh, eat together, and sleep in the same room was not the best sight. This is my father, and he is supposed to be doing this with my mother.

There's a physics principle that explains how two subatomic particles can be intimately linked to each other even if they are separated by millions of miles apart. This means that if you separate two subatomic particles by millions of miles and you observe them, if one at point A exhibits a certain characteristic, the other at point B will exhibit the same characteristic even though they are millions of miles apart. Whatever is happening to A is also exactly happening to B. Just look at one, and you'll know the other behaves the same way. Quantum Entanglement, they call it, but I call it the bond between two people in love, like my mother and me.

At night, I would lay in bed wondering what she was doing. In the song, 'Hello,' the singer, Lionel Richie, asked a question that crossed my mind a few nights about my mum because I was missing her, and it was as if a part of my heart was left behind.

Cause I wonder where you are

And I wonder what you do

Are you somewhere feeling lonely?

Or is someone loving you?

Everything happening was affecting me here in the US. In one room was my father and another woman having possibly the best time of their life. Yet, I felt back home that my mom was missing all of us and perhaps even feeling lonely. We have spent all our lives together, but now we are with the man who left her behind. It was just so bizarre. I didn't know if it was even good for me. At some point, I felt maybe I should have stayed in Nigeria. Perhaps we should just have stayed back.

When we were leaving Nigeria, we were so excited that we didn't take too many things. I remember we didn't travel with many clothes because we were so excited to relocate to America. We had many good clothes back in Nigeria but never went to America with them because we felt we would get new ones. We went with nothing apart from our traditional wear.

At some point, I felt maybe I should have stayed in Nigeria.

One of the reasons dreams are delayed and, sometimes, never fulfilled is because of a lack of required finances. It seems like our dreams would be hit by this effect, too. My dad had no job, which he didn't tell us, or maybe he did, but he didn't have money, and we didn't know. He didn't buy us clothes; consequently, we had to wear our native attires to school because we had registered for high school immediately.

My clothing was strange and off in the school. It made me stand out of the crowd. It made me so conspicuous that even a blind man could see me from afar. People would laugh at me. My brothers were embarrassed and ashamed. In a country where you were a person of colour, having one more thing to be addressed by was making everything worse. Thankfully, we spoke with our mom and explained everything happening to her. She wanted us to be comfortable, not because she had much, but because she knew these were her children and she had a duty to fulfil.

Mom bought some clothes from Nigeria and sent them to us. After a while, my dad decided to buy us some clothes. He took us to Walmart and got us some clothes. However, the dreams began to fade, and reality began to dawn on us.

Not too long after we got to the US, he married his girlfriend, passing the message to me that he had nothing to do with my mom anymore.

As time passed, we became a burden to him, like hideous vermin he wanted to eliminate. Suddenly, he became very harsh and strict with us. We used to wait till they had gone to bed before we ate. We dare not make mistakes, and we dare not fail. Life was not like other kids for us. We were not entitled to love, care, and patience.

I came here with hope, love, joy, excitement, and the desire to meet and know my father again. However, everything had taken a turn for the worse. Coming to see all of that chaos was tough on me mentally. It broke me into more pieces than a glass would if you smashed it against a rock.

I was young and came here to maintain that youthfulness, but life has hit, and this was no longer the time to be young. In his song, *'Put the Blame on Me,'* Senegalese musician Akon apologised for growing up too fast. But I can't apologise for mine because it was a necessity at the time. I had two brothers who were going through exactly what I was going through, and I know how they must be feeling watching their father treat them that way. They needed a hero. However, our first real hero, our mother, was a million miles away, so I had to be the new hero; I had to be our mother.

My brother and I became like orphans. Our mother wasn't here, and it feels like our father shouldn't. He was the thorn in our flesh. The man supposed to protect us was now the one we needed protection from.

My life began to mature swiftly, and all my innocence died because I could see through my father that the world wasn't all it seemed.

My mom was continents away from me, and my dad only wanted dastardly things to happen to us.

I knew I must protect myself and my siblings from his abuse one way or the other. Rapidly, I began maturing and began understanding anxiety, depression, anxiety, sadness, heartbreak, and deep sadness. I was deeply sad, didn't like my life then, and didn't have much motivation to do anything. Nothing inspired me. I was lost because I didn't have the guidance and love I needed to guide me. It was like I was all alone in this world.

My dad would rejoice at any bad thing that happened to us. If I didn't do well in a class, he would laugh at me, almost as if to say, I know you can't do well. Whatever made me sad made him happy.

He always wanted to use our failures to justify why he abandoned us all those years. He wanted to use our down moments as a 'didn't I tell you they are good for nothing' moment. He didn't bring us there for him to cater to us or watch us succeed; rather, he wanted us to fail while he had a front-row seat as he watched it happen.

For weeks and months, he waited for that big eureka moment to make him call my mom and say, 'Aha! I told you. Those children won't amount to anything in life.' Thankfully, it never came.

He would tell me that my beauty was all I had to my name, just like my mother. Tragically, he wasn't praising it; he was mocking it. My dad never wanted me to be happy with myself. He said that if he were a man, he would never want a woman like me. He said nothing was special about me, and just like my mom, we are all about beauty. Sadly enough, he never treated his wife any better. He told her to her face that she was not the most beautiful, but she was a nurse, so she had more value than me. This made me despise nursing, and I hated that he wanted me to be a nurse. He idolised that career and would rub it on my face, reminding me that my mom had failed because she hadn't gone to nursing school. My goal was then to prove I could succeed without being a nurse.

How he treated his wife made me pray and wish that he never reconciled with my mom. I asked my mom what she saw before marrying him because the person she had told us about was not the man we were living with. He never spoke well about anyone and couldn't even live peacefully and harmoniously with his siblings.

He would always talk down on his wife and even slapped her once. Their marriage was an example of what I didn't want, and my prayer point was that God should give me his exact opposite as a husband.

I felt my mother marrying him was a crime, and he was still the one to punish her for it. He verbally abused me so much that even when I wasn't around him, I could still hear his words echoing in my head. Each time I was returning home from an outing, I would begin to panic and get scared because I knew it was going to be another episode of living in hell.

The first few days in America were the only sane days we had. After that, it was like the gates of hell were opened, and the fire emanating from them burned badly.

He did many things I can't even mention because they were brutal and demeaning. But I remember asking him to drive me to the airport once because I was travelling. I hadn't been able to find my way around town alone, and it wasn't an era of Uber cars. There was only one of three ways to transport yourself. Either you drive, get driven, or find your way via the public transport system. I didn't have access to the first option; my dad was the only one available for the second, and I wasn't familiar with the third.

Consequently, I had no other option than to tell my dad to help me by driving me to the airport. I knew it wouldn't turn out well, which was why he was the last option I considered.

Sadly enough, he never treated his wife any better.

He told me I had to buy him gas and food. I promised I would if we could just get going. He agreed, and on our way, he branched at a restaurant called Red Lobster, where I bought him the food. He ate it all before taking me to the airport.

The citizenship

My mom was doing all the jobs she could in Nigeria to ensure she could send us money whenever needed. More often than not, we would outlandishly call her from the US to send us things. The burden was supposed to be lifted off her after we travelled, but the opposite happened.

My dad called my mom and told her about my brother's citizenship, which needed to be done. He told her he didn't have money and that time was running out. Immediately, my mom swung into action. I knew her salary was little, but she saved it all up within the short window my father gave her. Thankfully, she raised the $1,500 my dad requested and sent it to him.

However, my dad didn't do what he had collected the money for. Rather, he usurped the money meant for their citizenship and never filed it. When I asked him about filling for my brothers, he said he had used the money for personal effects. I asked why, and he said it's because my mom has been spending his money all these years, and he is paying her back. I couldn't believe my ears. I couldn't believe he was trying to get back at my mom at the expense of my brothers' future. This hurt me so much. However, it further taught me who the man my father truly is.

CHAPTER 7

THINGS! FALLING APART

"What do you call the opposite of dreams? Nightmares!"

Sandra Mbeyi

Life was supposed to be fun here; life was supposed to be a paradise here. If anything we dreamt was true, life here was supposed to be a haven. But everything here has been the opposite of our dreams. What do you call the opposite of dreams? Nightmares!

A few months before this very day, my dad had gotten me a phone. However, we were at a restaurant one fine evening when a call came in. It was my friend, so I excused myself and stepped aside to answer the call. My friend and I laughed over the phone. Out of the blue, my dad came fuming, grabbed the phone, shattered it by smashing it on the ground, and almost slapped me. If we were not in public, he would have. However, he pushed me. He was furious and said I was racking up the bills.

I had often seen him angry, but this was a new high. This wasn't the first time I made a call on the phone while he was around me, and he never got angry, but that was the first time he had heard me laughing over the phone. Furthermore, we were in public. Anything to embarrass me would be fine.

For a few weeks, I didn't have a phone or a method of communication with anyone, especially my mum. I knew she would be worried back home because she knew we weren't in safe hands. Now, our silence will seek to compound her fears even more.

But everything here has been the opposite of our dreams. What do you call the opposite of dreams? Nightmares!

Thankfully, that friend I was on the call with bought me a new phone. It was probably the first time someone who wasn't my mother had given me something I didn't demand or deserve. I got a new phone, and the price I paid for it was friendship. Whenever my mom got me things, the price I paid was called love, but whenever my father got me anything, the price we paid was my mental and psychological health. For just little things, the price I paid was steep.

Nothing I did was ever good enough. He assaulted me mentally, verbally, and psychologically. He would say some of the meanest things on this earth to me. For the record, the most demeaning things that have ever been said to me in my life were said by my dad. He said I was useless and dumb and also said my brothers would end up in jail and they would never amount to anything, even me. He even tried to break us up. He would tell me it was okay not to be close to my siblings. I wasn't surprised because when we came to the US, my dad hadn't spoken to his brother, who was in that same US with him, in five years. They later reconciled years later.

During our ordeals, I remember calling his brother (my uncle) because I was surprised we hadn't heard from him since we entered the United States. We never saw or heard my dad talking to him, and he never called us. I remember my mom advising me to call him. However, when I did, he told me he didn't want to have anything to do with my dad. His words were sharp and quick, "Once bitten, twice shy." Those weren't the only words he muttered. He said many other things, but I can't remember them all.

As a result of how my dad treated me, I didn't want to be with men. I became a loner and was always all by myself. I didn't even want to have any male friends or companions. I began to fear men and failure. I didn't want to fail because I didn't want him to say things like, "Didn't I tell you that she's good for nothing?" "I knew from the outset that you'll not amount to much?" I didn't want men because I didn't want to be abused and talked down on the same way my father did. I built an invincible fortress around me to keep the men away.

My dad had decided to further his education in the United States, so we had to take some classes together. I couldn't say a word or do anything because I didn't know how he would react to them. Furthermore, I didn't want him to embarrass me if I did something contrary to what he thought was right. I went to school in fear and couldn't do anything with my peers. The fear of my father embarrassing me publicly among friends and strangers was a nightmare. Even when it wasn't happening, the thought of it plagued me every time. The only time I was assured of not being abused was the moment I was in that instance. I was uncertain of what the next second held.

Eating at home was a problem because the house didn't feel like home, even though we could cook. This was not our mom's kitchen; it belonged to another woman, so we had to be careful. Furthermore, my dad would only buy what he could eat without caring about the things we could. As a result, we ate cereals a lot. It was the only food available under those circumstances. For many weeks, we lived on only cereals and water. My brother liked to eat, and my dad would complain he was eating too much and finishing his money. He once said it looks like my brother was sent to eat him broke. I told him this is how we eat, and we barely even ate much. Our mom fed us well back home; food was never monitored or measured.

School, snow, and bikes

Rocksprings is a small city in Wyoming, and the distance between our school and home was about 20 minutes. The weather was rough, and we only had about two months of summer. The rest was severe wind and snow. Wyoming was so cold that it used to snow up to six inches, and the cold affected us adversely. We came from a temperate region. We were within new territories where the weather and time zones differed from where we came from. The time difference between Nigeria and Wyoming was seven hours. So, whenever it was almost afternoon in Nigeria, it was early morning in Wyoming. Thankfully, our bodies were slowly and surreptitiously adjusting to its new realities.

We needed time and patience to blend into our new realities, but our dad would offer us none. My brothers had to wake up early to prepare for school, but on occasions when they overslept, they would be late for the bus, which left at 6:45 or 7 a.m. Once they missed the bus, they would beg our dad to take them to school, but he would refuse. It didn't matter if the whole country was quaking or if fire was falling from the skies; as long as they weren't taking the bus, they had to find other alternatives in a country they didn't know much about. Devastatingly, they dare not stay home. On days my brothers missed the bus, they had to walk to school under the freezing weather.

One day, my brothers missed the bus, and our dad refused to take them to school, so they had to walk all the way. A woman who knew them from the neighbourhood saw them on the road and exclaimed like she'd seen a ghost.

"What are you doing?" She bellows.

"We're just walking." One of my brothers responded quickly.

"Don't tell me you're walking to school?"

For a few seconds, my brothers didn't know what to say. But the woman knew they were walking to school. With a bag back and a winter jacket on, where else could they be headed?

"Get in, let me give you a ride."

My brothers entered, and the woman drove them to school.

He was supposed to be our father but had become our fear.

These incidents continued for weeks. If they missed the bus, they would have to take the long walk to school. Since our dad wouldn't take them to school on such days, they approached him to get them a bicycle. However, his words were like those from a stranger's lips. He told them he would buy the bikes but only on one condition. What condition? They asked. He told them it would be like lending it to them, and they would need to repay him. Back at home, in Nigeria, we had our bicycles. Maybe if we had known, we would have brought them along.

My brothers went to a different school, while my dad, his wife, and I attended the same school, so we always had to go to school together in his car. Those trips were the longest of my entire life. Thankfully, I had friends who would drop me off whenever he wasn't attending.

He was supposed to be our father, but he had become our fear. Whenever I missed one of the classes we took together, he would say bad things about me. All these affected me adversely because I wasn't expecting all these kinds of treatment from my father. There was a time when I went through an emotional depressive state in school and did poorly in my classes. The moment he heard of my poor grades, he didn't talk to me about it to know why my grades had gone from good to bad and from bad to worse. Rather, he called my aunt and told her everything. He told her I was failing, useless, and couldn't even pass my classes. He abandoned us for many years and was always looking for a reason to justify his actions, or should I call them inactions? He needed to convince himself that what he did was what we deserved. This is why he was very quick to announce our failures. He wanted to recruit others to his rank so they could love him and say that we deserved what he did and how he had treated us. He was always slow to celebrate our wins. Whenever my brothers and I did well in our academics or won awards, he would never call anybody to share the story with them as he did with the bad news, and he would never celebrate anything we did, no matter how little or big.

We were not allowed to make any mistakes. If we did, he would call my mom and tell her my brothers were bad kids and that we would not amount to anything. In fury, my mom was angry with him on the phone. He could abandon her or mistreat her, but she wouldn't allow him to talk down on her children without her having a word to say. That day, her words were angry and piercing.

"My children aren't bad. If they did, then you are the cause. You are the reason, and I'll hold you responsible for anything that happens to them. When they left here, they were well-behaved children. Also, those children are blessed, and they are not useless."

The outsider

Do you remember the verse of the Holy Book where Moses pleaded for the Israelites to be set free, and the Egyptian king made things even worse for them? I could say in this story that my mom was the Moses, my dad was the Pharaoh, and we were like the Israelites—enslaved and without a place to run to.

One night, after he had returned from work, he and my brother, Marvin, argued, and he kicked him out. We pleaded with him to let my brother stay in the house because the temperature outside was freezing, and he had nowhere to go. But all our pleas and cries fell on deaf ears. Marvin slept in my friend's dorm that night.

I could remember crying and feeling scared because my brother was away from home, devoid of safety, care, and attention. However, my dad didn't move an inch or care about his son's safety. Finally, our pleas were answered, but not until the following morning. He let him in, but with another plan in mind. I knew, left to him, he didn't want him in his house anymore, but he had to. However, that wasn't the end of the situation.

A few days later, he physically assaulted my brother again, and the whole house was as obstreperous as a flock of crow-blackbirds in their migration season. Everyone tried to wade in for him to stop, but this time again, all our pleas fell on vacant ears. Even his wife pleaded with him to stop, but he didn't listen to anyone. Instead, he went to the kitchen to pick up a knife and tried to stab my brother. Thankfully, Marvin was quick to make a run for it. I had seen him extremely angry countless times, but that day was the height of it. He was willing and ready to do the unthinkable without considering the consequences. Each time I look back, I ask what could have been if my brother hadn't run. What if! Just what if!! He survived that night only by a hair's breadth.

Sometimes, I would call my mum and tell her everything that was happening to us. But I didn't know how to tell a mother that her son was a split second away from death. How do I tell her that, added to all the punishment and torture we were facing, we were now also facing death threats? I didn't want to frighten her. She had already gone through enough.

I was young, but nobody cared about the things I needed. The only person who did was far away, and the one who was closer didn't care. He wouldn't even ask me if I needed anything. In a strange land, abandoned and without an income source or support, I had to devise ways to raise money to afford the things I needed.

I had to begin the frantic search for a job, and luckily, I got a part-time job at Home Depot and later with Herberger's. From then onward, I could afford some of my needs without much help.

When God wants to bless you, He sends people into your life. When the devil wants to destroy you, he sends people, too! It is you who must discern who has sent whom.

Sometimes, in school, we needed computers for our projects. I was lagging, and unfortunately, I couldn't afford it then. Aunt Mitzi, who was like a grandma to us, decided to lend a helping hand by assisting me in raising the money to buy my first computer, which cost about $200.

A few days later, my dad called Aunt Mitzi to brag that he had gotten me a laptop. However, unknown to him, she was the one who bought it for me. Aunt Mitzi smiled and just played along without uttering a word about it.

Aunt Mitzi was one of the greatest things to have ever happened to me. When I was about to crumble many times, she held me up. When I had nowhere to turn, she became like a compass. God knew how difficult this journey would be, so He planted her in my life to help me see it through. They say when God wants to bless you, He sends people into your life. When the devil wants to destroy you, he sends people, too! It is you who must discern who has sent whom. I believe God wanted to help, and Aunt Mitzi was the vessel He used to convey it.

I saved enough money through my job to get my first car—a Nissan Altima. It was small, but I didn't see it that way. I was so happy to get that car because going to school with my dad was torture. Walking those long distances under the sun, snow, and rain was as exhausting as it was scary. Finally, here comes solace. Small as it may be, it was a big relief because I was about to give up on school due to the difficulty it always took to get there.

Seeing I had bought a car, my dad gave me $20 to put gas in it. He said it was culture, and he blessed the car. He acted like our father for the first time in a long time. It was beautiful to watch, even if he could be this and even better than this. But don't be fooled by this act; he never changed. This was like a cheat day for him to do what a father ought to do because the days that followed were hot as hell. Thankfully, that car I bought was my saving grace.

CHAPTER 8

WHOSE REPORT WILL YOU BELIEVE?

"More often than not, books are a document of our victorious battles."

Sandra Mbeyi

The Holy Book said, "Who can speak and have it happen if the Lord has not decreed it?" This is why, every day, I thank God for my life. If I hadn't held on to Him steadfastly, I wouldn't have been able to write this book. They say books are a document of our victorious battles, which means if I hadn't held onto God, there would have been no victory, and without that, this book wouldn't exist.

The power of words

Words can tear down and build up. As someone once said, "Words have oppressed and liberated countless. It is a weapon that can inspire and save lives or discourage and forsake them." Scientific studies have also shown that positive and negative words affect us on a deep psychological level and significantly impact our lives because our words contain energy and power.

To counter his words, I had to develop perfection syndrome because of all the things he had told me.

Nathaniel Hawthorne said, "Words! So innocent and powerless as they are, as standing in a dictionary, how potent for good and evil they become in the hands of one who knows how to combine them." My dad had said many bad words to me, and I knew there were only two ways to ensure his words didn't come to pass in my life. I had to use a far greater word to counter it–God's Word. Furthermore, I had to act to make my life's outcome different from what he had conceived. Consequently, I kept trying to live my life to do the opposite of what he said.

To counter his words, I had to develop perfection syndrome because of all the things he had told me. I told myself I wouldn't settle for anything other than excellence and would always do my best in anything my hand finds to do. I would read like my life depended on it, work hard as if my whole existence would collapse if I didn't, and pray like it was the only way to climb the success ladder.

I kept praying to God to give me the resilience and strength to make my mom proud. God was my only hope, and I knew He would never fail me. This stone the builder has rejected must become the cornerstone.

I lived in all purity and diligence, and I wouldn't lower my standards or be caught doing any of those things he had tried to engrave on me. I strived to be anything other than promiscuous. I was diligent and had very high standards. I paid more attention to my actions than anyone else did, and I became my accountability partner. Even when there was no one to monitor or control me, I did it myself.

Immediately my brothers and I travelled out of Nigeria, it was like everyone back home had forgotten about us. We became nothing but memories. It was like we didn't exist. The moment we were out of sight, we were equally out of mind. Nobody, no relation, and no extended family reached out to us. Excluding my baptismal father, nobody ever called to check up on us. We felt rejected, unwanted, and abandoned. Yet, it wasn't surprising because even growing up in Nigeria was difficult without a father. Once you don't have a father, automatically, you would be termed an immoral kid and the community's black sheep. The world is more accepting of single mothers raising children alone now than it did then. Back then, growing up without your father present was frowned upon. You were regarded as the bad egg of the community, and parents even warned their children against associating with you. If I can use a word to describe it, I would say outcast.

I had all eyes on me, and all kinds of expectations were anticipated of me.

While I was schooling in Nigeria, I was bullied because they didn't believe my dad was abroad. They believed I was fatherless. When adults advised my peers to read their books, they would give us different advice because they felt we didn't have a father. So, they imagined we were more susceptible to vices than everyone else. In the others, they saw virtues because they had a father present in their lives. In us, they saw only immoralities.

Everyone could talk to me and say whatever they wanted. I was open to everyone having an opinion about my life. I often compared myself to friends and cousins who had present fathers, and I observed many differences in how they were treated and approached because they had a covering. When the others were told to read, I would be told not to be a bad girl, not to join bad gangs, not to follow boys, not to get pregnant, and not to draw tattoos. They assumed the worst of me and all of these because I didn't have a father.

We were often mocked and overlooked, sometimes out of ignorance and other times jealousy. My dad will often send us clothes from the US, and my mom ensured we always all wore it out together.

I would never forget the day I wore a beautiful dress to church and excitedly, I showed my uncle after church service. I was excited and spirited, but all those positive emotions would disappear when he rather mocked me and said, "All my dad does is send clothes but he will never come home to see us." I was young and excited, but that day, my little heart was hurt and I never forgot that statement. All I wanted was to show him my exceedingly flowing gown but he wasn't interested and he never smiled back. He also made many more indirect mockery statements and they hurt me more. It was like inflicting a cut and adding salt to the wound.

I also had a bosom friend whose mom told to stop being my friend because children raised by a single mother were bad kids. Well, if only my dad was around.

A father is supposed to be a child's covering, especially a girl-child. He is supposed to be her first love and her first lesson. As someone once said, "Dad, a son's first hero and a daughter's first love." However, my brothers didn't have that hero, and I didn't have that love. I didn't have that cover, and I was denied that lesson.

Consequently, I was exposed, vulnerable, and prone to all sorts of things life threw at me. Naturally, as a child, some things must go through your father before it gets to you, like insulin, which regulates the amount of glucose in the body. However, the lack of insulin causes diabetes in the body. My dad was supposed to be that insulin, but since he was absent, I was becoming metaphorically diabetic.

In my father's absence, I held on to God because that was the only pillar my mom had introduced us to. At a young age, even before things fell apart, she had already introduced us to Jesus, and I knew he was there for us and with us, even when walking through the valley of the shadow of death.

I prayed to God and worshipped Him because I knew He was the Father of the fatherless and our last hope, but I knew I needed a deeper relationship with Him. I needed my identity to be rooted in Him. I needed to embrace Him. I was lost, and I needed Him to find me.

Thankfully, just as the electric pressing iron converts electrical energy to heat energy to fulfil the purpose of its creation, I converted all the happenings into propelling energy that inspired my drive for success.

I had nowhere to run but only one place to turn: God. I often listened to worship songs. Then, I'd pray, and thankfully, I had friends who stood by me. Friends I could call anytime to talk to.

CHAPTER 9

IT'S A MIRACLE

*"Every successful step you take and every challenge you overcome
are miracles."*

Sandra Mbeyi

My life was like a swing, which was being controlled by externalities. I was young, but I had to become old quickly. I was innocent but had to step out of my comfort zone. I wanted to be lifted, but I became the pillar. Everything was robbed off from me. Sophia Loren said, "When you are a mother, you are never really alone in your thoughts. A mother always has to think twice, once for herself and once for her child." This was what became of me. I needed people to ask questions, and I needed to be taught. At that age, I needed to be one of life's students. However, fate won't deem it so. As a result, I had to grow up quickly.

I began seeking answers to things I didn't know and became one of life's teachers. I did all these because of my brothers. They were younger than I was and needed guidance and direction. Since there was nobody else to provide them for us, I had to take the metaphorical bull by the horns.

The ousting

I woke up one morning and told my dad I was going to Nigeria to see mom. I had missed her, and I knew she had been alone for a while, coupled with the fact that we had had no good news to share with her since we got to America.

As I gazed at the rising sun, I wondered why my life had no much fun. I said I would go and meet the one person I could share everything with. The one person who could feel my pain as I felt it and empathise with me as I desired. I was weary and tired and needed to rest my weary head on her strong shoulders. I needed to draw strength from somewhere, refill all my used energy, and assure my mom that everything would be fine.

He said I should not return to his home the moment I leave.

However, immediately I whispered into my dad's ears about my envisioned visit to Nigeria; his words were stern and quick. He said I should not return to his home the moment I leave. I was stunned and scared. However, on second thought, I felt peace within. Maybe I could finally live a peaceful life. Instantly, he told me to leave his house. Conceiving the idea of wanting to see my mom in Nigeria while I was in his house was, to him, a grievous crime. My mom had become the fictional Lord Voldemort in the popular Harry Potter series—a person whose name you do not mention—a name he doesn't want to hear. So, I moved all my luggage out and headed back to Nigeria.

When I returned to Nigeria, I finally saw my mom for the first time in a long time. My eyes lit up as a flood light, and no scale on earth could measure the joy I had within, not even the Ritcher scale. Seeing my mom was one of the most beautiful sights ever. I could have sworn she looked like the most beautiful thing I'd ever seen. It was lovely to see someone who loves you for you and feels your pain the way you would. The last time I felt loved was when I left the shores of this country, and it was from my mom. However, thankfully, I'm back in her warm embrace, feeling it again—that lovely feeling of a mother's love. As someone once said, "I am nothing without my mother. She is the reason for everything I am and all that I will be."

Our holiday was wonderful. Spending time with my mom and taking a break from all the heavy blows life had dealt me in the US was splendid. It felt like heaven. Devastatingly, this beautiful holiday will be cut short by news from my brothers in the US.

Marvin and Kevin called me and said dad had kicked them out, and they had nowhere to go. All the wonderful feeling in me thawed instantly. The vine within me was blooming, but those words turned it gloomy.

My brother, Marvin, and my dad were always at loggerheads. Marvin missed mom and would always want to talk about her. However, my dad wanted to ban that name and word from his house. As I said earlier, he wanted my mom's name to resemble the fictional Voldemort.

One night, my dad and brother, Marvin, were having their issues again. However, he would ensure this misunderstanding would be the last between them. He looked at him and said you are leaving this house this evening. My brothers were about eighteen then. He told Marvin to pack his luggage and leave the house. Marvin's twin brother, Kevin, was stunned. He looked at our dad and said, "Why are you sending him out? Where do you want him to go? You know we don't know anybody here."

He looked at Kevin and roared, "Why are you begging? I don't understand. Do you think he's the only one leaving this house? You are going with him, too. All of you should leave my house."

Marvin was surprised and muttered. "I was thinking I'm the only one you have an issue with, why him? What has he done? He has always been the good child."

The one begging had become the victim, and the first victim had become the one begging. The question now is, who will supplicate for them? My dad hardly ever listened to anybody.

He screamed and asked them to leave his home. It felt like a dream, but it was real. It felt like it wasn't true, but this would be our new life. At a young age, and in a strange land, my father threw out his sons in the middle of a freezing night. Where do they go? Who do they call? Should we be surprised he's doing this, or should we have expected this from him? We were lost between both worlds. On the one hand, we were surprised, but on the other hand, we couldn't have expected more. My brothers were out in the cold while our father was under the shelter in the warmth of his bed and had no care for his children's welfare.

I was carrying more load than I could bear, but I dared not crumble because everything would fall apart if I did.

Back to Wyoming

Immediately I heard the news, my trip turned sour. Everything was beautiful for a while, and the noise of life had been shut out. Suddenly, everything was about to be altered. Life was about to hit me again. I changed my ticket and began planning my return to the USA. He accused my brothers, who had never stolen, of stealing his camera. They told him they had never touched his camera, but he insisted they stole it.

So, that night, I begged a friend of theirs to house them for a short while till I returned. Thankfully, he accepted, and they slept on his couch till I returned with some money my mom gave me. However, I never told her anything because she would be beyond worried. The smile my presence had put on her face was immense. It had been long since she was happy to that extent, and I didn't want it to be shortlived.

When I got to the United States, my brothers and I rented a motel for a few days while we looked for money and a place to lay our tired heads permanently.

House on wheels

We had nowhere to go and knew nobody else in the US besides my dad. We couldn't return to Nigeria because my mom would be heartbroken. Furthermore, we were pursuing our education, and we couldn't abandon it at that point. I couldn't even call our mom because she would be scared and worried if she ever found out, and I didn't want that scenario. Like a shock absorber, I had to absorb and dampen all the shock impulses from getting to others—my mom and siblings—

not knowing that absorbing all those things inside and processing them alone was also not healthy for me.

Whenever my mother called to cry that she heard what our situation had been, I tried to downplay it and assuage her fears. I knew she would be feeling helpless and devastated knowing her children were walking through the valley of the shadow of death, and she wasn't there to walk through it with them. However, she knew that no matter the situation, a fourth man was in this fire with the three of us.

Whenever my brothers were also going through hell, I wouldn't allow it to get to my mom because I knew she would lose sleep, and that would be dangerous to her health. I became the confluence where all problems met. I was carrying more load than I could bear, but I dared not crumble because everything would fall apart if I did. I had to be strong, and I had to be the bond. At this point, more than ever, I had to be the mom of two teenage boys.

After our payment at the motel expired, we packed our luggage into our car and left. We kept driving even though we didn't know where we were going.

We drove through the town but couldn't find any place to stay, both downtown and uptown. So, instead of driving the car around, we thought, why don't we just make it our home? Finally, we parked at a gym facility. We would sleep in the car at night and go in to take a shower at the gym in the morning. Then we drove off to wherever we had to go. I will drop my brothers at school before driving back to work. At times, whenever it was possible or if it was too late at night, we would park the car at a soft spot and pass the night there. In the morning, we would drive to the gym again, use their shower, and go about our day. We used the Wi-Fi at Home Depot or McDonald's whenever we needed to use the internet. The little money I was earning at work was what we used to feed.

The most devastating side was that there was nobody to call for help. I couldn't tell my mom her children were living on the streets of a strange country she hadn't been to before because I couldn't imagine the torture it would bring to her. Knowing your children are somewhere suffering and hearing their voices but not being able to do something about it has to be the worst torture a mother can go through.

I was stretched mentally, spiritually, psychologically and physically; if this force continues further, I might break, and I might collapse.

I worked extra hours to make more money and avoid being in the car too early. I overworked myself and barely rested. It was like I was elastic. I was stretched by life, but I kept on stretching. Physics tells us that elasticity is when a body resists a distorting influence and returns to its original size and shape when the acting force is removed. However, even elasticity has limits. If you stretch it beyond its elastic point, it will break. If you keep applying the force that makes an elastic stretch continuously, without halting, the elastic body will break. Sadly, life wouldn't take a break from applying the distorting force stretching every part of me. I was stretched mentally, spiritually, psychologically and physically. If this force continues, I might break, and I might collapse. Sadly, that wasn't the scariest part of it. The most devastating part is that my meltdown would have a domino effect on my brothers and mother. Like a pack of cards, if I fall and can't carry on anymore, it would cause a catastrophic collapse for everyone. They would all fall, too. At that point, I felt like the fabled Atlas. The Greek myth depicts him as carrying the world on his back.

My family's survival was resting on my feeble shoulders. We came all this way to chase a dream, to pursue our education, and to make a good life. But all these dreams now rest on the shoulders of a young girl. I had to carry the cross and wasn't allowed to drop it yet. I was overstretched beyond the limit, but I must never break. As Maya Angelou said, "You may encounter many defeats, but you must not be defeated. In fact, it may be necessary to encounter the defeats so you can know who you are, what you can rise from, how you can still come out of it."

I encountered many defeats but must not be defeated while remaining strong and steadfast. I wouldn't deny the fact that I needed help. Somebody, save me. Help me with my cross.

The accident

Life is unpredictable. It is fickle and can be altered within seconds. The distance between life and death is a matter of fine margins. In one second, everything could be over as it would have on this very day without God's divine intervention. Whenever I tell people that I can't live my life without serving God, it's because, without His intervention, I wouldn't even be here. He brought me this far via miracles.

I once needed to travel, so I told Marvin to take me to the embassy to put certain things in place. However, the only embassy was about three hours away from our city. So, he had to drive me there. Furthermore, the heavy snow and weather conditions made the road slippery and frozen, making driving a tad difficult. Our going was smooth, but our car slid and almost fell into a ditch on our way back. Our car was just an inch away from tilting over. It was at an equilibrium at the ditch's edge. If our movements weren't well calculated, the car would tilt forward, and we would go downhill. My whole life flashed before my very eyes. I held my breath for a while because, at that point, it felt like the world had ended.

My God! We were just an inch away from falling into a ditch, but the car suddenly stopped there as if something had brought it to a halt.

The first thing I thought of was God helping us through, but the first words I muttered were cries for help. "Marvin! Marvin!! Marvin!!!" I screamed, although not as much as I should have under the circumstances.

Thankfully, he was on hand to pull me out. "I got you, I got you; I got you." He said, trying to allay my fears. Little did he know that I had been to heaven and back. For a few seconds, my soul had left my body and returned.

My God! We were just an inch away from falling into a ditch, but the car suddenly stopped there as if something had brought it to a halt. Other road users stopped, parked their cars, and came down. Even they were worried and rushed towards us, asking if we were okay, to which we responded in the affirmative. Although still reeling from the close shave we just had.

Even they couldn't believe we were okay, but we were. We walked out of the car with no scratches, bruises or any threatening injuries. The people around helped, and we continued our drive home.

At that point, I knew my mom was praying for us, and God was with us because what happened that day was a miracle, and it helped to boost my confidence that God was watching over us. Each time I look back, I still can't explain how we survived. It was nothing but a miracle.

The Graduation

Out of something bitter would come something sweet. From a situation that was supposed to crumble us, we would turn it around to build something beautiful. My brothers were finally about to graduate. Even though we were homeless, it didn't stop them from moving on to greater things. Mavin and Kevin finally graduated from high school.

Kevin cried that day, saying he wished our mom was here to witness the graduation.

I had to go to work on their graduation day because I couldn't take time off. So, they bathed in the gym after we had all slept in the car that night. After that, I dropped them off at school for their graduation.

Kevin wept profusely that day, saying he wished our mom was here to witness this beautiful day. His heart was broken beyond a million pieces, and our mother being present would have made it more beautiful. Thankfully, they still graduated with magna cum laude. They had so high CGPAs that when the school called them out, the students went wild in jubilation because they were so intelligent and athletic. It was a day filled with happiness and joy.

Our day of joy, our day of honour, and our day of glory. We were born in a small Isiokpo village in Rivers State, Nigeria. We grew up in the capital city of the state known as Port Harcourt, but here stand my brothers, tall and heroic in Wyoming, United States, covered in praise and basking in their momentous euphoria. A beautiful sight and a wonderful achievement accompanied by ostentatious applause. Only if our mom was here and our father would have loved us enough to witness such a day with us.

A gas miracle

Roy T. Bennet said, "Believe in your heart that you are meant to live a life full of passion, purpose, magic and MIRACLES." I can say boldly that I believed in these four elements he mentioned. If not for them, I wouldn't be here today, especially the miracles. My life was one big miracle, and it was always evident in every event that happened to me.

Our car was our home; it was a house on wheels. As a result, we needed so much gas to power it because we were on the move a lot.

Wyoming was a cold region then, so we had to always keep the car on to stay warm. However, sometimes we had no money for food, not to mention gas. Most days, we usually bought $10 or $20 worth of gas. However, we had no money that day, and it was cold. Since the car was how we got warmth, we had to keep it running so we wouldn't freeze. When we checked our pockets, we had nothing. It was $0, and we needed that car to keep running, or else we might freeze to death.

In that instant, I was disturbed and knew a miracle had to happen if we were to survive that night in this freezing cold. In faith, I decided to drive down to a gas station in downtown Wyoming. I got the fuel nozzle and put it in our car. Surprisingly, fuel came out, and I filled the tank without the machine asking for my card or cash. Each time we were out of cash, we would go there and miraculously fill our tank. However, one day, I tried it when we had some money, and it didn't work. This was proof that God saw and was watching over us, helping us at every point.

I couldn't even explain how it happened. Well, I believe it's a miracle. As John Blanchard said, "A miracle is by definition beyond the ability of science to explain and must also therefore beyond the ability of science to disprove."

My life was one big miracle, and it was always evident in every event that happened to me.

A SERIES OF FORTUNATE EVENTS

When we left the shores of Nigeria, we did so with the hope and possibility of something special happening. Although we were reluctant to leave Nigeria, we left with hope coursing through our veins. An old African proverb says, "Hope is the pillar that holds the world." However, this pillar was crumbling before me.

Finding solace

One of life's most important things is shelter and we lacked a good one. We had been living in the car for weeks, and I concluded it wasn't safe for us. Furthermore, the temperature in Wyoming was harsh and freezing. Consequently, we needed to get a place to stay and fast. I contacted many friends to help me with accommodation, but none was forthcoming. After a frantic search, a friend, or so I thought, asked me to come and stay at his place for a while. Nobody else would allow us to stay with them except him. At that point, I didn't analyse or think twice about the offer. I was only excited that we finally had a place to stay before we froze to death.

He said I could bring my brothers, and they could sleep on the floor, so we went. I slept with him on his little twin bed while my two brothers slept on the floor. The night was going smoothly for a while. Having a bed and a warm shelter felt good once again. I couldn't even remember the last time we had such luxury. A bed and warmth were luxuries for people who had spent months in their car under the cold. However, this treat will be made ephemeral that same night.

While I slept like a baby, I felt a hand on my hip and flung it. He repeated it. I held his hand this time and asked if it was because he offered me a bed that he felt he could assault me. He said he liked me and other things I didn't listen to. He tried to force himself on me that night, but I mustered all the energy in me to repel him till dawn.

At the first show of light, I told my brothers we were moving out. It wasn't the best news to them, but they always trusted my words and instincts. They knew when I said let's move; it was time.

We moved out of there and back to the car. Thankfully, shortly after, we raised money and got a trailer-style one-bedroom flat. Finally, we had our space and bed, and I became a full-time mom. I would cook, take care of the home, and ensure they woke up early for school. I was their new father and mother.

I didn't tell them any of the things happening at the time because I wanted to protect their mental health. So, like a mediator—a guarantor—I stood in for them. I did everything I could to guide them and ensure that their mistakes as young adults did not stick with or derail them. I fought for them, defended them, and took everything that was supposed to be thrown at them and absorbed it. I stood as a wall and ensured what was on the other side of life didn't get to them, a colander to ensure the hard parts were sieved away before they reached them, and an umbrella to protect them from life's scorching sun and heavy rain. I was the one being beaten down and feeling most of the effects of what I was protecting them from. Tragically, no matter the intensity of a burning fire, the wall never runs. It must do what it is meant to do, even at the expense of burning down.

I was being their mother instead of the cool sister like every other sister they saw.

We had our issues at first because I had a watchword and passed it down to them. They didn't see me as a cool sister because I didn't allow them to go out and be involved in all the misdemeanours associated with youthful exuberance. I was their mother instead of the cool sister like every sister they saw. I needed to live in a way that would positively influence them. I didn't want them to see me living a wayward and irresponsible life.

Do what I say, not what I do, is the anthem of hypocrites, and I didn't want to be one because then, I wouldn't be able to advise them, and they wouldn't be able to respect me. They won't be able to listen to me. **Matthew 23:3** admonishes us to practice what we preach, "So practice and obey whatever they tell you, but don't follow their example. For they don't practice what they teach." I didn't want to be like that. I didn't want to be a talker, but I wanted to be a doer.

Consequently, I dedicated my youth to living a life my brothers and mom would be proud of. The whole time I was in the US, I only went to a party once as a single girl.

Some of my friends mocked me. They would tell me to get dressed and go out with them to party. However, I always declined. I couldn't because I wanted to set good antecedents for my brothers.

It caused friction initially because I didn't allow them to attend parties. I wanted them to avoid making any mistakes under my watch. Whenever I asked them to do something, and they didn't, I would call our mom, and she would chastise them over the phone. To them, I was the annoying sister. I abstained from all vices and all forms of promiscuity. Throughout our stay, my brothers never saw me with any man and neither did I bring any home.

Furthermore, on days I wasn't working, I was always in before the moon was out. Even though I was in charge and in control of my life, I felt I had to be accountable to my brothers and lead by example. I couldn't enjoy my life because of the fear of making mistakes; atelophobia, they call it. I was just there hoping God would reward me one way or the other in the future.

I was unfazed by what was happening around me. I just kept living my life irrespective of whatever my peers thought or said. It was easy for them to judge me because they didn't know my situation and what I was going through. As they say, "Don't judge someone until you have walked a mile in their shoes." But they tried to judge me without walking in my shoes to see how heavy it was to move in.

Financial aid

Marvin and Kevin were admitted into Western Wyoming College. Unfortunately, we couldn't afford the fees. The only way they could attend the school was through financial aid.

Financial aid is money received from the government to help students pay for their education. However, it wasn't for everyone. You had to meet certain criteria, which we didn't meet.

Our dad registered them in school the first time we got to the United States. As a result, the financial aid department will judge them based on my dad's information and how much he makes. If the earnings on my dad's statement were above a certain threshold, my siblings wouldn't qualify for the financial aid. Sadly, when they crosschecked my dad's records, it was above the requirement. They didn't qualify by that rule, even though my dad wasn't in their life or paying their fees. This means my brothers couldn't attend college because we couldn't afford it, and nobody was available to sponsor them.

At that point, we had only two options: forfeit the admission or go and plead with our dad to send them to school. I wasn't sure he would listen to our words. We only needed one other thing: God's divine intervention—a miracle.

We began hoping and praying for a miracle because it was our last resort. My brothers still filled out the form, and I went to the financial aid office to speak with them. I spoke with the man in charge, and he told us we could use our mom's information and that he would help us. I couldn't believe my ears. This was supposed to be impossible; this had been called undoable. One more time, God has made a way where there seems to be no way.

I didn't believe it until the man called our mom in Nigeria, interviewed her, and used her information instead of our dad's. It wasn't supposed to happen, but God made it happen. Miraculously, without knowing anybody and without going back to beg our dad, God raised helpers to ensure our dad's actions and inactions never halted our life's momentum.

That man helped my brothers qualify for financial aid. Additionally, he was in that school till they graduated. Surprisingly, he left the school after their graduation. I don't know if it was of his accord or if he was transferred. I believe God kept him there to be a helper throughout their stay in that school. I believe God sent helpers ahead of us. He knew we were young, innocent, and were being led like sheep to their slaughter. However, He was already there to shield us. We walked through water and didn't drown; we walked through fire, and the flame didn't kindle upon us. I'm not the mother of Dragons, but you could call me the unburned, and you wouldn't be wrong.

Emergency room

May Sarton said, "Loneliness is the poverty of self." Furthermore, **Genesis 2:18** says, "It is not good for man to be alone." Companionship is a vital aspect of human life. I call it one of life's most vital necessities. However, I learnt the importance of companionship in the hardest of ways.

I woke up one morning feeling pangs of pain in my stomach. I tried to shrug it off and go on with my day, but it proved to be something I couldn't. Marvin and Kevin were in school, so I was home alone. Suddenly, the pain intensified, and I could barely move. It was as if life was leaving my body. I picked up the phone and realised that I had nobody to call. The only family I could call–Marvin and Kevin–were miles away. I instantly dialled 911 to report my emergency. However, the last thing I remember was what I told the first responders on the phone. "Help!" From that moment, I remembered nothing anymore.

Thankfully, the emergency service arrived on time to pick me up from my bathroom floor and rushed me to the emergency room. Then they called Kevin to come. In a flash, he rushed down to the hospital. He came to the emergency room and saw me lying there like a wet vegetable. He was scared because we knew whatever happened that day could have had a more sinister ending. If I had been a split second late, I wouldn't have been able to call the emergency number. If I hadn't, the outcome could have turned out to be gory, probably a call to glory. But glory be to God that I could call for help before blanking out.

Immediately I got better, I knew I couldn't live alone, and I had to leave Wyoming. Marvin and Kevin were safe in school, so I had to search for my safety. But I believed living alone might jeopardise it. So, I had to find a safe place.

The Houston debacle

They say the end of a statement is the beginning of another. The end of one journey is the beginning of another. When you solve one issue, it is nothing but the beginning of a new one. The Biblical King Solomon puts it wisely when he said, and I will paraphrase, there's nothing new under the sun.

Everything is running in circles. I've learnt that life isn't a sprint; it's a marathon. Devastatingly, you must keep sprinting in this marathon of life to stay ahead.

I wanted to put issues of the past behind me. However, unknowingly to me, what was ahead was as problematic as what had gone behind. Sadly, that's the tragedy of life. It doesn't matter how bleak or uncertain tomorrow is; time will ferry you there. Once again, time is about to ferry me to a new challenge. I wished time could pause so I could breathe a little, but it turns out, in life, there's no breathing space, just a recovery phase.

I left Wyoming and moved to Houston without having any plans. I didn't have any tangible strategy when I moved there. I didn't know where I was going or what to do. I had a male friend who used to live there in Houston. So, before I got into town, I had called and told him I needed a place to lay my head. Thankfully, he said I could come to stay at his place, where he lived alone. Finally, I had a place to rest my weary eyes because they had seen the gates of hell. I went to stay at his place. Tragically, I had only stayed there for one night before the situation became chaotic.

When I arrived, he had another friend travelling through Houston who needed a place for the night. He told his friend to sleep on the couch. Initially, I had wanted to sleep on that couch, but his friend was to sleep on it. So, he said I could stay on the floor in his room. However, I told him I'd stay on the other couch, which he approved. In the middle of the night, he sent me a text. "Why don't you want to come to bed?" I responded with another text. "I'm fine on the couch." So, he sent me more messages. He asked what was wrong with me and my plan for him, and when I was coming, did I think he would just give me accommodation in exchange for nothing? That night, he sent many other incessant superfluous messages.

It wasn't what I had expected and wasn't even within the scenarios I had imagined. So, I told him, "I know you're engaged to be married. Consequently, I never thought you had such dastardly things in mind for wanting me to stay with you. I felt it was from your heart's goodwill."

Not again, and not tonight, I muttered to myself. Immediately, I called my mom's friend and told her I had to leave where I was because I was no longer feeling safe. She told me she would come the following day, which was a Sunday. So, I had one more night to spend there.

When his right hand touched my body, I jumped and roared like a wounded lion.

The next day, after his friend left the house, he must have licked his lips and thought the window of opportunity had been wide opened. So, while I was sleeping, he made that attempt again. I wasn't deeply asleep because I had it at the back of my mind that he could decide to attempt it again, and this time, it would go beyond texts since it was just the two of us in his apartment. I was hoping for the best that night but expecting the worst. Tragically, my expectations were met; he didn't even disappoint. He crept up to me slowly, but immediately his right hand touched my body, I jumped and roared like a wounded lion. "What's wrong with you?" I asked angrily.

Before he could speak, I jumped out of the couch to avoid anything forceful and headed to the safest part of the house in times of trouble—the exit. I called my mum's friend and told her I had to leave this place urgently. Sunday was near, but it was now looking too far away.

She could read even the things I wasn't saying. My breath was shaky, and my voice cracked like an antenna with a bad signal. Thankfully, she came to see me and took me away from there instantly.

I told her I needed somewhere to stay, but she couldn't offer me a place because of where she was at the time. However, she helped me find a lady looking for a nanny for her son in exchange for accommodation. The woman didn't pay me any money for my work. All she gave me was accommodation and barely any food. I didn't mind any of the conditions because the most vital thing I wanted had been granted—a place to sleep. Having it was enough. I lived with her, helped her clean, made food for her son, took him to school, picked him up after school, and took care of the house chores. All these were in return for an accommodation. Sometimes, she would leave her son with me to travel to Nigeria. Only the boy and I would be at home. Yet, when she returned, there would be no news or sign of trouble or mischief. Even the boy didn't mind his mom travelling for long days because I made sure I catered to him immensely.

However, his mother wasn't reciprocating my wonderful treatment for her son. I've always believed that the best way to make a mother smile is to make her children laugh. Sadly, it turned out I was wrong.

I would call my mom's friend and complain about how I was being treated, working hard yet having almost nothing to eat. She would try to pacify me by telling me to endure until I could figure everything out. I had no choice but to keep living with the condition I was in. The only beautiful thing about that place I worked as a nanny was that it was devoid of an impending rape danger. Where I was before, I was in danger of being raped. So, even though she wasn't paying me, I was okay just being there. Safety is a valuable commodity, and I was happy to have it, even at that cost.

...she called my mom and told her to send her the money for everything I ate and the repainting of her wall.

However, she called me one morning and told me she and her son were relocating to Nigeria. As a result, they wanted me to leave their home. I hadn't figured out where to stay, and this development came out of the blue. It meant I had to immediately begin sorting out housing issues again. Sadly, my biggest immediate challenge wasn't even accommodation.

The woman told me I had to pay for all the food I had eaten in her house. She also said she saw a lipstick stain on her wall, which she assumed came from my makeup. As a result, she assumed and accused me of staining her wall. Within a flash, she demanded I pay for the wall's repainting. Before I could say a word or even plead my innocence, she called my mom in Nigeria and told her to send the money for everything I ate and repainting her wall.

Thankfully, my mom did. She sent the woman all the money she requested. However, she didn't allow me to go until she received it. Immediately after she collected the money, I left her house, never to return.

Extended stay

Back in Wyoming, my brothers were supposed to attend the school for two years, but they stayed there for four years, to the point that the school became their permanent address. That was the only place they knew as home and the only safe place they knew. By the end of the fourth year, the school began providing them with counselling and therapy services. They told them they needed to graduate because nobody was supposed to be in the school for more than four years, and they had been there for that duration.

The school called my brothers and asked why they were extending their stay. They asked if they were scared of the world and life?" The response was a resounding yes. However, there was no way the school would allow them to stay beyond four years, so they told them they would be fine.

Still, my brothers didn't want to leave, but the school chased them out. Finally, they graduated and left the college.

CHAPTER 11

A NEW HOME

I can't remember the last time I had fun or felt extremely happy. There were many human emotions to experience, but I could only feel a few–heartbreak, devastation, and anxiety, albeit tainted with a bit of hope and a mixture of faith.

After I left the house where I had worked as a nanny, I decided not to call my mom's friend again. I knew she stretched herself before getting me that place, and I no longer wanted to burden her with my life challenges. I believe we all have personal life trials to deal with, and I didn't want to add mine to hers. I was willing to carry my cross myself.

I decided I would go stay with another male friend. Based on my last experience staying at a guy's place, I would have loved a different place. However, I had no other choice. There was nowhere else to go, nobody to call, and nowhere else to sleep. I had a male friend who became my last resort. I either had to take my chances with him or risk sleeping on the road and being vulnerable to vicious crimes.

One of my happiest moments was when I got my brothers to experience the big city for the first time since they arrived in the United States.

He took me in, and I stayed with him for a while. Thankfully, he didn't try to harass me. I felt comfortable at his place, got a job, and even saved some money. I was missing my brothers so much. So, while I was at his house doing some jobs, I was able to raise money to fly them to Houston so that they could see a big city for the first time. One of my happiest moments was when I got my brothers to experience the big city for the first time since they arrived in the United States. Finally, they could have some fun in a life that hadn't provided them with many. We visited some fun spots and beaches, which was a happy moment. They stayed with me for a while. Sadly, it was when my brothers came to Houston that I knew my friend had become a different person. He tried to take advantage of my trust. When I refused his advances, he stopped being kind to me. Consequently, I began making plans to leave his place. After everything, my brothers returned to Wyoming, and I went to Maryland.

A new sojourn

Change is inevitable, and my friend had fallen into this inevitability. When I refused his advances, he stopped being the person he had always been. Before things got out of hand, I began looking for a place to stay. As God would fate it, my uncle called and told me his family had just moved to Houston, and he would need somebody to help stay with his wife, keep them company, and help them. I had prayed covertly, asking God to help me leave where I was unscathed, and He answered overtly.

So, I went to stay with his wife and kids while pursuing my acting career in Nollywood movies, plaiting hair, and doing makeup. The desire to further my career took me to Maryland, USA. I stayed with my mom's best friend when I got there. Once again, I had someone to share my experience with. The night I told her everything was the first time she knew about what we had gone through. We sat together that night for hours as I explained all we had faced. We spoke till about 3 am, and I watched as she wept copiously. The knowledge that we had gone through that much pain shattered her heart beyond a million tiny pieces. She felt aggrieved that she wasn't there to go on the journey with us, and she apologised for not being there during our trial days. I stayed at my mom's friend's place for a while and bonded with her kids. For the first time in a long time, it felt like things were beginning to shape up.

After my stay in Maryland, I flew back to my uncle's house in Houston. Finally, I was having a settled life. I've had a troubled life until then, but something big was about to happen. I graduated from the University in Texas, and for the first time, my brothers, mom, and I would be together and hold each other in America. My mom flew to Houston for my graduation. Her visit was as miraculous as it was enthralling. A few years before that very day, my dad called my mom on the phone and told her there was no way she would enter the United States because nobody would bring her. He also said that there was no way she would be able to afford it. So, her arrival was like breaking a jinx. As **Lamentations 3:37** alludes, "Who can command things to happen without the Lord's permission?"

I flew my brothers in also to be a part of the celebration. Things were beginning to take shape, and I had nobody else to give glory to but God.

Some weeks later, a friend visited while I lived at my uncle's house with his wife and children. We said a lot, but within the tenets of our conversation, I deviated and echoed my situation. I spoke to her about my situation, and she told me her family had a house in the city. I asked if I could stay there, and she agreed. They weren't living there then; they lived in Nigeria but had a home there. So, she allowed me to stay in their home temporarily.

While I was in Nigeria, my mom told me that my dad said my brothers were behaving badly in the US and were in a lot of trouble.

So, while I was there, I kept doing my business alongside other jobs. Eventually, I raised some money to rent a one-room apartment in a couple's house. They were wonderful people, and they treated me like family.

Homecoming

Even while we were away from our father and things were beginning to take shape, he hadn't taken a break from talking about us to people, especially our mum.

While I was in Nigeria, my mom told me that my dad had called her and said my brothers were behaving badly in the US and were in a lot of trouble. Consequently, they won't be able to come back to Nigeria, or they will be jailed. My mom was scared and almost in tears. The fear was palpable in her voice, even in how she spoke. I told her it was untrue and nobody is seeking to jail my brothers. Even though she believed me, she still thought I was trying to allay her fears by downplaying the gravity of what was happening. To make her know it was untrue, I raised some money and added my savings, which amounted to about six thousand dollars ($6,000). Then, I, alongside my brothers and aunt, planned a surprise visit to Nigeria for them without my mom's knowledge.

We were having a normal Christmas celebration, but I could see that my mom was worried about my brothers. Like an absent piece from a puzzle, it was conspicuous to see that she was nervous about them. It felt like her celebration was incomplete without knowing if they would be able to visit Nigeria one day.

On Christmas Day, December 25, 2014, my brothers arrived in Nigeria without my mom's knowledge. She was at my aunt's house when I went to pick them up at the airport. My mom had no idea they were the ones we were going to pick. When we brought them back home, she saw them, screamed at the top of her voice, and was beyond excited. She had almost lost hope of seeing them soon based on what my dad had told her, but here they stood. I watched my mom cry the tears of pain and joy combined. The tears were from the joy of seeing them again, even after she had been told she wouldn't. "I thought they said I can't see my kids." She yelled at the top of her voice. "I'm so happy to see my sons once again. Thank God I'm alive to witness this day. They said my sons can't come home again or they will be arrested and jailed, but here they are. Thank you, God."

That day stood as one of the most emotional and fulfilling days of my life, watching my mum weep profusely in both joy and pain. Finally, she saw her sons in Nigeria in good health, and all the rumours she heard were confirmed to be false.

My aunt, brothers, and I brought a genuine smile to my mom's face, and the happiness in her was unfathomable. We were responsible for her joy, and it made us happy.

Houston and beyond

The first time I left Nigeria for the United States, it was with mixed feelings. However, this time, I left Nigeria and returned to Houston with elation. My brother's visit to Nigeria brought indeterminate joy to my mom, and I was infected with it. Seeing her happy, smiling, and celebrating was one of the most beautiful pictures my memory holds dearly. I was a proud and happy daughter who was grateful to God for using her as a vessel to bring a smile to her mother's face.

After leaving Nigeria for Houston, I began planning to bring my brothers to come stay with me in the city permanently. I called my uncle and told him I was planning for my brothers to move to Houston. He was against it. He told me I hadn't even gotten my ground and was already thinking of my brothers. He insisted vehemently that I consider myself for the interim. But I couldn't. So, I searched for a school for them in Houston.

Thankfully, my mom visited the United States while I was searching for this school, and we drove there to make our inquiries. When she saw it, we both agreed it was good for them. Plans began earnestly for them to move to Houston. At long last, Kevin and Marvin moved to Houston.

Financial aid (Another miracle)

Challenges are an integral part of life. They come in various forms, such as personal losses, health issues, financial difficulties, or relationship struggles. However, understanding that these challenges are inevitable helps us adopt a realistic mindset towards life. It also gives us the strength to always carry on. Henry Ford said, "When everything seems to be going against you, remember that the airplane takes off against the wind, not with it."

When my brothers moved to Houston, another financial aid challenge arose. Marvin needed financial aid from the school. However, his department told him he wasn't qualified for it. That was a problem because we knew we couldn't afford the school.

For him to qualify for financial aid at the time, our parents needed to be citizens of the United States, and my mom needed to have her social security number while meeting other criteria. Dejectedly, my mom wasn't a US resident yet, so she didn't have the number. Once again, the impossible stared us in the eyes. If my brother were to move forward in his academics in that school, that financial aid mountain had to be removed. Thankfully, the Holy Bible in **Matthew 17:20** teaches us the only way to move mountains. "...I tell you the truth, if you had faith even as small as a mustard seed, you could say to this mountain, 'Move from here to there,' and it would move. Nothing would be impossible."

This was an impossible that needed to be reversed, and with faith in God, the impossible would become possible. So, we held on to the only thing that could help: faith in God! As **Zechariah 4:7** alludes, "Nothing, not even a mighty mountain will stand in Zerubbabel's way; it will become a level plain before him…"

With nothing else left to do, we just had to use our faith to show up where our case would be decided. My brother stood no chance, but like Queen Esther in the Holy Book, we showed up and received divine favour out of the blue. When we got there, they met a woman who was so good to us throughout the admission process.

There were procedures to follow, and they were stringent. Thankfully, though the process was difficult, this woman kept working round the clock to ensure my brother had an alternative. To make the impossible possible and to continue his education, this woman miraculously helped him, and he got financial aid to finish his education in Houston.

CHAPTER 12

FINDING GOD; FINDING LOVE

"Whose report will you believe? The one God has ordained or the ones people wish to be true in your life?"

Sandra Mbeyi

My mom imbibed in me the fear of the Lord. She taught me the right way to go when I was living with her in Nigeria; even when I lived without her in America, I didn't depart from it. I hid God's words in my heart to ensure I did all that was good.

I had been able to scale many of life's hurdles, although I hadn't reached the finish line just yet. To be fair, even when you feel there's no more hurdle left, life always has one in store for you. As long as we live, there will always be something to overcome. Thankfully, I knew this early in life.

Furthermore, even when my mom wasn't with us, I trained myself to be a good daughter who would make her proud and not be caught doing things that wouldn't make her happy. So, before I got married, I became a wife. I imbibed the qualities of a good wife, which endeared me to many honourable men.

Subsequently, when it came to suitors, there were different men who were mostly out of the country, and they would travel from far away and try to court me. Some were trying to take giant steps into marriage. I had never positioned myself as a girlfriend or had that mindset, which endeared me to all the men who came around. However, while they had their sights on marriage, I would spend the time carefully trying to get to know them. One thing my dad's experience taught me was definitely what I did not want in a husband. It was because of him I began praying early about my future husband. I didn't want a man like my father, and I never stopped reminding God about it every time. I would tell God on countless prayer engagements about the loving and caring man I wanted. Thankfully, He answered.

I prayed fervently about my future. It was like my life depended on it. I didn't want the aphorism: "When we get to the bridge, we will think of how to cross it." I want to start thinking about crossing the bridge before getting to it. One thing about life is that the future begins today. The future you desire has already begun.

I made a list of the qualities I wanted and needed in a man and prayed with it. I told God I desired a man who would love and cherish me. I said all the prayers for the future, then. This had been my routine from age fifteen.

> *Even as a young girl, I was preparing myself for the future.*

When I met my husband, I told him I was in a covenant with God. He was the first man I told. I told him I was already predestined to have a great marriage, and if he was not the chosen partner to embark on the journey with, then it wouldn't work. I also told him I knew God dwelled in and within me through the Holy Spirit, so pre-marital sex was a big NO as it was a big part of my covenant with my Father. He agreed to everything with no hesitation. I later came to find out he had also begun seeking the face of God, as did his mother, and they both got their convictions pretty quickly.

When I saw and heard people around me talk bad about marriages when I was young, and the experience of my parents' marriage. I would mutter to myself, "There had to be more." There are good marriages, and mine would follow that trajectory. I always said I would never settle for less.

My uncle once told me that what I wanted in a man was too much and that I should get ready to settle because the sort of man I wanted didn't exist. "Mould that kind of man you want!" He would passively insinuate. He said a woman has her prime, and once I'm past it, I will start praying for a husband. He told me not to raise my bar, to settle for whatever comes, and to choose quickly.

However, avoiding the kind of man my dad was even led me to choose some wrong men for a while. I was walking and living in fear, and what I dreaded kept happening to me. I knew I had to move my mind from fear to faith.

I started a relationship blog, listened to many relationship teachings, and read books about relationships and marriage. I learnt and practised many skills. I started an event company, and I learned makeup and hair braiding. I also tried to act in movies and even became a writer. I wrote for other blogs before I started mine. I wrote about many things, even a letter to my future husband. I did all this to ensure when the right man came, I would also be the perfect woman.

*When I was young, my mom taught me to read
books, especially Christian ones.*

As the Bible says in **Proverbs 22:6**, "Train up a child in the way he should go, and when he is old, he will not depart from it." Also, as they say, "Catch them young, and they will be yours forever." Whatever you show your children when young will most likely stick with them forever.

When I was young, my mom taught me the essentials of reading books, especially the Christian ones. She bought many Christian books and materials for me. Therefore, continuing on that pathway was easy because she already set me on the path to follow, so I kept moving along that line. It made me love Christian books, blogs, and shows. Thankfully, they began teaching me a lot about marriage.

Prayers, therapy, prayers

Seek, and you'll find. In furtherance, I began to seek healing and ways to ensure every hurt I carried was wiped off. I decided to visit a therapist. It was a transformative therapy session. It was so emotional as well as exhilarating. I read my life to her like an excerpt from a best-selling novel. I didn't know when I busted out crying and screamed. I poured everything out from my heart amidst profuse tears. The therapist couldn't help but cry with me. The journey of my healing began that day. I knew there was heaviness inside of me. What I didn't know was that there were layers to it. That very day, I told myself my healing had begun.

I kept talking to God, telling Him I knew His words would come to pass in my life. On the other hand, my mom did not relent. She kept sending her prayers into my future. She would cry to God, go to the altar, lay on the floor, rolling, crying, and praying. She would fast and pray for days for God to take control of the situation. She would take my picture to the altar and leave it there. She would cry and pray about my marriage so much that I just knew I couldn't marry wrong.

Still, I kept praying without ceasing. One thing I never did was let go of God's hands. I always held on to Him. I would always seek His face, and I was active in church.

My mom's script

Thoughts and ideas aren't exclusively unique. This is why if you tell someone to think of a place they've never been or describe something they've never tasted or seen, they can't. Our thoughts, words, and actions are from what we've seen, heard, tasted, and experienced. There were thoughts in my head emanating from the life experience I was trying to purge. However, a young man approached me one morning with a note from my wild experience.

I wasn't moved by all he said because I kept remembering my mom's experience.

The young man was from the same village I came from and said he wanted to marry me. He told me he had prayed about it, and God told him I was his wife. He narrated how he saw me in a dream and how I've now become the literal girl of his dreams. This is Deja vu because I have heard it before. This was exactly what my dad told my mom. Those words began something passed down to me, and I promised myself it would end with me. My children will feel my love and their father's, too.

I wasn't moved by all he said because I kept remembering my mom's experience. Like a movie, it flashed right before my eyes. However, just because it was like that with my mom doesn't mean that approach will always have that outcome. Yes, our thoughts and ideas come from what we've seen and heard, but I decided I won't judge him by what another man has done. I will judge him by what he is, not what I assumed. So, I told him I would pray about it. I have read the Bible repeatedly, and I know God rarely talks to one person without talking to the other, except you are disconnected from Him, and He has been trying to reach you fruitlessly. When God spoke to Apostle Paul, He spoke to Ananias; when He spoke to Apostle Peter, He spoke with Cornelius; and when He spoke to Elijah, He spoke to the widow. Even when He spoke to the Virgin Mary, He spoke with Joseph, too. Unless you are lost, God doesn't do one-sided conversations. So, if that's what God told you, sir, I believe He will tell me the same when I ask. God is not an author of confusion. So, if He's speaking to you, He would speak to me, too.

So, I kept praying about it, even though we kept talking and trying to get to know each other. However, while doing that, I introduced him to my mom. For the first time, my mom would say she doesn't like someone and doesn't approve of us going forward together. With no affirmative answer from God, everything collapsed, never to see the light of day.

Finding destiny

Some great things in life are discovered by probing, finding, and experimenting. Some are discovered by accidents, like Quinine and Penicillin. Furthermore, while we look elsewhere, life will always find a way to get our attention, as it did in 2016 when I met the man who would later become my husband.

When we first met, he was a regular guy to me. I wasn't thinking about marriage or relationships. When I met him, I told him I wasn't interested in any relationship. However, his response was bold and sharp. He said, "Whatever God wills must surely come to pass." He wasn't pushy or disturbing; he was rather highly confident.

A few days after we met, he started calling me Nneoma, which means good mother. I thought it was the weirdest thing ever. I even tried to get him to stop because I couldn't understand why he was calling me that name. Of all the sweet names that exist on earth, he chose to call me Nneoma. But only God knows what he saw in me that made him call me that name. I never liked the name that much then, but now I appreciate it more than anything, and it has taken over my real name, Sandra, and my nickname—the girl. He doesn't call me anything else, just Nneoma.

I started seeing good qualities in my husband. I went to meet my pastor and told her what was going on. I told her two men were showing great interest in me. While my husband sought my hands in marriage, another man wanted to enter the picture. So, I wanted to know what God's will was. My heart leaned towards the man who finally became my husband, but

I needed to hear from God first. I wanted to move by faith, not sight, to ensure it wasn't an idol of my heart.

My pastor told me to pray about it and fast for a few days, which I did. I prayed, fasted, and told God to show me a sign and ensure my future husband was revealed to me. For no apparent reason, the other guy went cold on me. We did not argue, fight or agree to stop seeing each other. He just went silent and never bothered to call or check back. I thanked God for helping me to sieve the weed away from the wheat. I had always had the spirit of discernment. I've trained myself to hear from God, see His signs, and listen to Him. So, I saw it as a sign from God.

The Devil can make rich, too, but the difference is that it doesn't come with peace.

So, when he wasn't talking to me, I got to know my husband more deeply, and we started forming a stronger bond. Furthermore, the more my husband knew me, the more he wanted to marry me immediately. However, I was praying about it even more. I didn't want to marry a man like my father, and I didn't want to make the same mistake as my mother. I kept asking God if this was not His will, He should reveal it to me. However, if it was his will, let it work out. Though, I have always felt peace about my husband from the beginning. There was no stress, drama, or chaos. There was no thinking and no calculating. It was just peace that supersedes all understanding. **Proverbs 10:22** says, "The blessing of the Lord, it maketh rich, and He addeth no sorrow." The Devil can make rich, too, but the difference is that it doesn't come with peace. Only God can give you the things you desire in addition to peace. So, the peace my husband brought was my cue that this was him.

He went to meet my mom, and thankfully, he was warmly accepted. My mom called me after he left and said, "I like this guy. My spirit likes him. But I'll pray about it." As the Bible Psalmist said in **Psalm 42:7**, "Deep calleth unto deep." So, I assumed their spirit clicked.

However, my mom began praying. She met her pastor, and they prayed, prayed, and prayed. Everyone had approved of him, but all that mattered to us was God's approval. Thankfully, God approved of our union. That was when I began giving him the real green light and all the audience he wanted.

Within a short period, he had gotten to know me and understood where I was coming from and my life story. However, he loved me more. It was as if God called him to love me. It was almost as if God anointed him specifically for my life.

The proposal

On June 18th, 2017, my husband proposed to me and asked me formally to marry him. My response was simple, sweet, and direct. 'Yes', I screamed with a heart full of joy and a face filled with smiles. I have had a turbulent life filled with many of life's tempests, but here, finally, God is saying peace and that I should be still.

Everything went smoothly from that point. We saw God's hand in everything, financially, spiritually, and physically. Everyone wanted to know who my husband-to-be was. Everyone had a word of advice for him. Knowing my story, my mom's story, and what I had been through, nobody wanted me to get married and suffer. Nobody wanted a repeat of my mom's story.

Days before our grand wedding, my family members kept buzzing in his ears that if he knew he was not real, he should leave me alone because I had been through a lot, and what I deserved now was love, care, and affection. However, my husband kept assuring me and everyone that he was for real. He promised them he would love and treat me well, and he made many other promises. To the glory of God, he has kept every single promise till today.

Cold feet

Edgar Allan Poe said, "We loved with a love that was more than love." My husband and I epitomised this maxim. Since we were beyond certain this was it, we began planning our wedding. However, two days before my introduction, I developed cold feet. Thankfully, my father figure took me on a ride in the middle of the night, and we talked extensively. He made me see so many things from a father's standpoint. He made me understand a lot, and he told me to go and see my mother-in-law the next day so that I would feel more at ease. It was what I needed, but something I didn't have—a father's reassuring voice that everything would be fine.

I heeded his advice and went to Umuahia to see my mother-in-law. I spoke with her extensively, and immediately, I felt like a stone had been lifted off my chest. It was like I had a blocked nostril, but now I could breathe freely. I felt peace after seeing my mother-in-law, and I was now more willing than ever to proceed with the wedding. I knew I was making the right choice, and his mom cemented everything for me on that visit. She was an angel in human form.

The introduction happened, and the wedding plans began almost immediately.

The nuptial knot

Before my wedding day, I had lived for it; I had groomed myself for it before it came. Before I married or met my husband, I had become a wife. While God was pruning me, He was moulding my husband, too. He was preparing him, and eventually, He anointed him to love me. My husband came and loved me like a father, a brother, and a mother. He took every broken piece of my heart and mended it.

> *Different people had many things to say, but they didn't know my husband like I did.*

I was a completely healed woman before the journey into marriage because my husband had loved me in ways I could not comprehend. His love was God's love in human form. He loved me with the love of God.

When we knew we would get married, I told my husband to call my dad and inform him that he wanted to marry me. I know he hadn't been in our life, but he is still my father, and he ought to know I would soon be married. My husband called him with a heart full of hope and joy. However, all these emotions dissipated when my dad told him he could have me for free, that I was worthless, and that he wished him well. He also called his kinsmen and told them not to accept my husband's drink. However, they told him they weren't a part of whatever happened between us. So they were able to accept the drink. Thankfully, his kinsmen supported me during the whole marriage process.

However, my dad, his siblings and their children never attended our wedding or bothered to check up on my husband and me, except for my dad's little sister. She attended and did her best to play the role of an aunty.

My mom went to my dad's elder sister with drinks, hoping she would change her mind about appearing, but she still didn't attend because my dad didn't. Same with his brother. I am unsure why they chose to treat their niece like that because of something they weren't a part of. My cousins had no regard for me, but why would they when my dad threw us to the wolves?

A few months later, my dad attended my registry marriage and attempted to be in our life. He said he never told anybody not to attend my wedding, and he is unsure why they did that. Shortly after my dad showed up, his sister called and apologised to me for not attending my wedding.

During the wedding, people who knew different aspects of me, especially how I was cynical about marriage and men and how independent I had to become to survive and support my brothers, were worried about how I would cope with marriage. However, they didn't know I was healed and changed.

Different people had many things to say, but they didn't know my husband like I did. They didn't see God's hand like I was seeing, and they didn't see the process like I did. So, I didn't pay attention to all those words because I knew I was fine. After all, God was with me.

It was not until after my wedding that the reality dawned on me. I was married to the man of my dreams, and every evil pronouncement on my life had been squashed. All my years of abuse had become a thing of the past.

God is truly Jehovah El-Roi and Jehovah El-Shama. The whole time, He was not only seeing me but also hearing me. While I was struggling, He was developing my husband for me and planning the outcome of my life. As **Jeremiah 29:11** alludes, "For I know the plans I have for you," declares the LORD, "plans to prosper you and not to harm you, plans to give you hope and a future."

The new miracle

Lamentations 3:23 says, "They are new every morning, great is thy faithfulness." Every facet of my life has been a miracle, and to date, the miracles have not stopped; rather, they are renewed every morning. Each time I face a brick wall, a mountain, or a seemingly impossible situation, I would pray for a miracle, and it will arrive.

Right after our wedding, I got pregnant, but I lost it. It was devastating, but we knew it was only a test of our faith and love. Thankfully, we stood firm in God's words, and He did it again for us. On June 18th 2020, exactly three years from the day my husband proposed, we were blessed with our first daughter. Someone once said, "The day a child is born, a mother is also born." That was the day the mother in me was truly born. Before the arrival of my first daughter, I was a wife, even though my husband always called me Nneoma—the good mother. However, the day I held my daughter's hands for the first time, it felt like I had shaken hands with paradise. The joy was immeasurable, and the thrill unquantifiable. From the South, West, North, and East, everyone was excited about this news. My husband and his parents, my mom and my siblings, everyone was elated. It was one of the best moments of our life.

Not just her birth that made everything profound, but the circumstances behind it added to the elation. Cesare Pavese said, "We don't remember dates; we only remember moments." The day I gave birth to my first daughter is one I will forever live to remember because she was a miracle delivered to us by God.

During my daughter's pregnancy, I suffered hyperemesis gravidarum—a condition of severe morning sickness associated with severe nausea and vomiting during pregnancy. I felt quite uncomfortable. However, through it all, my husband was my superhero. He supported me, and when I was so weak and tired and threw up, he would clean it up, bathe me, carry me, dress me and cook for me. He would be the one to drive me to work and still pick me up. He dedicated his life to taking care of me. When the baby came, he stepped into fatherhood. That was when I knew I was truly blessed.

I'm jealous of how wholesome my daughter would be because of the kind of father she has. She has one who would love her unconditionally and forever, just as Christ loves us. I believe every woman deserves that kind of father who would love you with everything he has.

I suffered from postpartum preeclampsia post-dural headaches after I birthed my daughter, but my husband stood beside me, holding my hands all through. I looked at him and muttered, "Wouldn't you go see your daughter?"

"Not yet. I want to make sure my wife is fine." He responded firmly.

…I was so close to suffering a stroke.

He didn't go until they cleaned me up. That was when my husband went to our daughter, carried her, and danced with her. I felt weak and tired and couldn't get up from the bed to join them in their father-daughter dance.

Another miracle happened that day. God sent this nurse, whom, to this very day, I'm still looking for. But nobody has any record of her. Nobody knows her name or anything about her. Just out of the blue, she appeared exactly when I needed her. I had developed complications from my childbirth process, and she happened to walk in when my condition was getting worse. She saw me, called another nurse in a fury, and told them to check my urine, which they did immediately. That was when they found protein in my urine. Before we could blink an eye, about five nurses rushed in. They began administering magnesium drip, which saved my life because I was so close to suffering a stroke. Each time I was seconds away from disaster, something that seemed supernatural would come to my rescue. When I was in danger, I could feel God's presence. Science has called it the third man syndrome, where during a crisis and emergency, people see, hear, or feel the presence of an additional person who doesn't exist or was never there. The third man syndrome, they call it, but I call it the fourth man in the fire. I call Him God.

My recovery was long and hard, but thankfully, my husband was very supportive. He took care of me alongside some friends God planted in my life. However, since it was the middle of the Covid era, my mom could not be there.

A new song

My life had improved drastically, and my marriage had become my blessing. My daughter was beautiful, but I wanted her to have a brother. Once again, I ran to the only person that has been rescuing and watching over me since the day of my birth. His name is Jesus; His name is God. I begged God again, had a conversation with Him in prayers, and told Him I needed a son. He honoured me again, heeded my call, and blessed me with a boy. I promised I would tell the whole world about everything He had done for me and still doing. My marriage has become a testimony, a yardstick, and a prayer point for people.

People have told me all kinds of things. Still, the greatest was when someone told me she could never doubt God's existence or power because my life radiates God's authority. This has always been my prayer point that my life glorifies God and that people look at the details of my life and see God written all over it. I've always prayed that God will use my life as a show-off tool to prove He is the mightiest. So, whenever people tell me things like that, I remind God of our covenant. Even my husband told me he would submit himself to God to be used as a tool to be a blessing in my life. He told me on our wedding day that our marriage would be a reference for good marriages. He told me he will not allow himself to be found wanting in loving me as God helps him, and he has not gone back on any of his promises.

Sometimes, I pinch myself to make sure this life is real and if it's mine. I have almost forgotten all my struggles and do not regret them because now I see through it all that God is good. All the events that were a part of my story led me to where I am today. I would not be who I am today without my story. It didn't kill me, so it made me and everyone better. As they say, "What doesn't kill you makes you stronger."

I remember my dad yelling at my brother one day when he was singing at home. He told him that he should go to America's Got Talent if he could sing. Years later, my brother stood on the big stage in America's Got Talent, though not to sing, but he stood there. He is a chemical engineer as well as a global celebrity. His twin is also an engineer; most importantly, they became men of good character. They were not influenced by my dad, which I feel was the reason God allowed him to kick us out. God didn't want them to become like him, so he removed them from under him. Sometimes, the bad things that happen to us are for our good, but we are humans, so we don't understand God's ways. As the Holy

Book says, "Everything works together for good to those that believe in Him."

Eventually, it makes sense. Thankfully, my brothers and I are still a formidable team, and the best part is that they now have another brother for whom they are grateful. My family continues to make people say, "Wow! God is good."

A small girl birthed in the village of Isiokpo, made from dust but elevated by God. He saw me through everything and heard everything in my conversations with Him. From nothing to something, God has raised THE GIRL!

My gratitude

We always prayed in Nigeria that God should bring my parents back together. But after I lived with my dad in the United States, I told God that if my prayer request letter was still with him, He should have an angel tear it into pieces, burn it, and throw the ashes into an abyss. I thanked God those petitions of mine weren't answered. Little wonder even the Holy Book said in **James 4:3a**, "And even when you ask, you don't get it because your motives are all wrong..." I was praying for what I wanted, but God knew it wasn't what my mom, my siblings, and I needed. By not answering that prayer, He was protecting us all.

If my dad had been in our life, I wouldn't have become who I am today, and neither would my mom have been the mother she became, filled with love, because she would have been damaged. I've never heard my dad speak well about anybody. He would say anything to you without any care of the impact it would have on your mental health. All he does is put people down, so I believe he would have destroyed her mentally.

However, as God wants me to, I have forgiven my dad and will always love and pray for him as my father. I was convicted by the Holy Spirit to always pray for him, so I always do. This is simply my story. My journey and my truth on how the woman you see today came to be!

FINAL WORDS

I give thanks to God for everything He has done for me. My experiences were painful and unpleasant, but I never knew God was using them to train and prepare me for what He had in store for my future.

God used all those experiences to shape me. Like a diamond, the fire I went through was to purify me.

The wisdom garnered from my experience is what I now use to run **Coach Next Door,** which was founded to inspire and mentor girls globally. The movement was born from my experience, and today, it is my ministry.

Only God's mercy has gotten me this far. Everything He has blessed me with, I do not deserve. I'm thankful, grateful, and contented.

Furthermore, it doesn't matter what you are going through or the challenge you are facing; my advice is that you hold on to God. If God has not given up on you (and He won't), do not give up on yourself or God. His track record proves His faithfulness. Whatever you are going through now is just a journey; it is not your destination. Don't let go of God's hand. He defies logic. He is a great planner and strategist.

His work and ways can be unusual, but He comes through. Give Him time and trust Him because He's faithful, and His mercies endure forever.